1,000,000 Books

are available to read at

Forgotten Books

---

www.ForgottenBooks.com

Read online
Download PDF
Purchase in print

ISBN 978-0-282-55391-3
PIBN 10856461

This book is a reproduction of an important historical work. Forgotten Books uses
state-of-the-art technology to digitally reconstruct the work, preserving the original format
whilst repairing imperfections present in the aged copy. In rare cases, an imperfection in
the original, such as a blemish or missing page, may be replicated in our edition. We do,
however, repair the vast majority of imperfections successfully; any imperfections that
remain are intentionally left to preserve the state of such historical works.

Forgotten Books is a registered trademark of FB &c Ltd.
Copyright © 2018 FB &c Ltd.
FB &c Ltd, Dalton House, 60 Windsor Avenue, London, SW19 2RR.
Company number 08720141. Registered in England and Wales.

For support please visit www.forgottenbooks.com

1 MONTH OF
FREE
READING

at

www.ForgottenBooks.com

By purchasing this book you are eligible for one month membership to ForgottenBooks.com, giving you unlimited access to our entire collection of over 1,000,000 titles via our web site and mobile apps.

To claim your free month visit:

www.forgottenbooks.com/free856461

* Offer is valid for 45 days from date of purchase. Terms and conditions apply.

English
Français
Deutsche
Italiano
Español
Português

www.forgottenbooks.com

Mythology Photography **Fiction**
Fishing Christianity **Art** Cooking
Essays Buddhism Freemasonry
Medicine **Biology** Music **Ancient
Egypt** Evolution Carpentry Physics
Dance Geology **Mathematics** Fitness
Shakespeare **Folklore** Yoga Marketing
Confidence Immortality Biographies
Poetry **Psychology** Witchcraft
Electronics Chemistry History **Law**
Accounting **Philosophy** Anthropology
Alchemy Drama Quantum Mechanics
Atheism Sexual Health **Ancient History**
Entrepreneurship Languages Sport
Paleontology Needlework Islam
Metaphysics Investment Archaeology
Parenting Statistics Criminology
Motivational

The Arte of Angling
1577

Edited by Gerald Eades Bentley, with an

Introduction by Carl Otto v. Kienbusch, &

Explanatory Notes by Henry L. Savage

Princeton University Press

Princeton · New Jersey · 1958

Copyright, 1956, 1958, by Princeton University Library

All rights reserved

L. C. Card 58-8561

Second facsimile edition

First facsimile edition published
under the sponsorship of
the Friends of the Princeton Library
through the generosity of
Mr. Carl Otto v. Kienbusch

Printed in the United States of America
by Princeton University Press at Princeton, New Jersey.
Facsimile text printed by Meriden Gravure Company,
Meriden, Connecticut,
from the copy in the Carl Otto v. Kienbusch Collection,
Princeton University Library

Design by P. J. Conkwright

Contents

Introduction

When 'Omer smote 'is bloomin' lyre,
He'd 'eard men sing by land an' sea;
An' what he thought 'e might require,
'E went an' took—the same as we!

The above "we" of course includes that long apostolic succession of those who over the centuries have produced the literature of angling, and the ancestor of all good present-day books on angling in our language is *The Treatyse of Fysshynge wyth an Angle* by the legendary Dame Juliàna Berners (or Barnes), which is thought to have been written some fifty years before it burst into print (1496) via the second edition of *The Boke of St. Albans*. My friend David Wagstaff, who bequeathed what is doubtless the outstanding library on angling in America to Yale University, was willing to defend by the hour his theory that Juliana Berners was a man, a certain Julian the Berner, keeper of hunting dogs on a feudal estate. A mere theory, however, should never be permitted to rob a lady of eternal fame. Whoever the author may have been, these twenty-three pages set the pattern for hundreds of volumes that fill our shelves. The *Treatyse* falls into three parts. The first sets forth the superiority of angling over other forms of sport, the second lists the items of an angler's equipment and gives instructions for their production and use against certain fishes, the third is devoted to the mental, ethical, and spiritual qualities found in the perfect angler.

[1]

The Arte of Angling

One hundred and fifty-seven years later appeared Walton's *Compleat Angler*, that lovely bucolic idyl, the most famous book in all the literature of sport. Dr. George Washington Bethune, editor of the first American edition, calls it "this darling book." How many have read and loved it is anybody's guess. Walton used the Berners pattern, developed and amplified, but not to an unrecognizable degree. He took what he needed from the writings of his predecessors but, being an honest man and a pious one, he tried to give credit where credit was due. Over the years Walton has been canonized as the angler's saint, the source of knowledge where fishing is concerned. His elevation to this pinnacle has been achieved to a large extent by those who have not read his book. Walton added almost nothing to what was already known, his experience being limited. Bait fishing was his proper sphere. He never caught a salmon and what he learned about fly fishing was mostly at second hand. What makes his book unique is the charm of its style and the picture it paints of Walton the man—simple, honest, wise, compassionate, God-fearing, lover of nature and of his fellow men, revelling in the innocent joys of his favorite sport.

If Walton ever had in his hands a copy of Dame Berners' *Treatyse*, one would expect some mention of it in *The Compleat Angler*. None can be found, though the *Treatyse*, according to Westwood, went through some sixteen editions and reprints before Walton's birth. Besides what I have called "the pattern," he was, however, indebted to the *Treatyse* for the twelve dressings of

Introduction

trout flies which Dame Juliana recommends and for some of the baits which she devised. These came to Walton through *A Booke of Fishing with Hooke and Line* (1590), largely and clumsily pirated from the *Treatyse* by Leonard Mascall. Mascall made mistakes in listing Dame Berners' flies and Walton copies his errors. Mascall is, however, not without honor among us, for, when writing from personal experience, he made worthwhile contributions to the technique of our sport, such as his suggestion that flies can best be prevented from sinking by applying a layer of cork along the hook—a shock to many of us to discover that this bright idea is over 360 years old.

Walton quotes at some length part of one of the best poems ever written on sport, *The Secrets of Angling* (1613) by an author whose name he gives as Jo Davors. The work was, however, entered on the records of the Stationers' Company as the production of John Dennys, March 23, 1613. It is largely didactic, but how much of Dennys' instructions Walton found useful is hard to say. It seems more likely that the poet helped Walton to appreciate the beauties of nature and the fisherman's joys so perfectly expressed in *The Compleat Angler.* Walton may also have borrowed from the notes appended to the second edition of *The Secrets of Angling* (1620) edited by William Lawson, for it was known to him, and Lawson was, for his day, a very advanced fly fisherman. If only we had a book by him on angling! It would doubtless be of great importance.

Walton was, moreover, acquainted with *A Dis-*

course of the *General Art of Fishing with an Angle*, first printed in *The Second Book of the English Husbandman* (1614) by Gervase Markham, an attractive rascal who made a living by writing on all sorts of subjects and selling and reselling the material under different titles to various publishers until they grew tired of being imposed upon and forced him to sign an agreement to sin no more. He had no scruples about turning Dennys' poem into prose, adding something from Mascall and perhaps from Lawson, plus something of his own, and selling the result as an original textbook. But what is actually original is good and an advance on what had gone before. His own outstanding contribution is in the matter of flies. He took Mascall's list, revamped it, added new patterns and advised that they be dressed to look as much as possible like natural insects.

Shortly before the appearance of *The Compleat Angler*, there was printed a little book which, in its first edition, has become one of the rarest titles in angling literature: *The Art of Angling* (1651) by Thomas Barker, a cook by profession; by avocation an excellent angler. He makes no pretense to writing "Scholler like" while boasting with a certain sly humor of his ability to fill his creel under difficult conditions and prepare his catch to perfection for the table. After reading a few pages you cannot help liking the man, one of those people you take to on short acquaintance. Walton thought very highly of him and admits borrowing large slices of his text: "I shall next give you some directions for fly fishing, such as are given by Mr. Thomas Barker, a gentleman that hath spent much time in fishing; but I shall do it with a little variation." Barker is the first to mention the reel, the first to give detailed instructions on how to proceed with the dressing of a fly, and advises "fine fishing" with the fly riding high on the water. He tells us that a skillful angler, like himself, should be able to land, on a line tapered to a single hair (no doubt from the tail of a white stallion) the largest trout—to do this, he must have used a long and limber rod. But what above all else endears Barker to the present writer is his passionate devotion to the art-science of cookery. Once for the guests of his employer, Admiral Lord Montague, he prepared trouts in broth, calvored trouts, marinated trouts, boiled, fried, stewed and roast trouts, trout pies hot and cold, etc. How the noble gourmets survived this gastronomic onslaught is not recorded, but one may surmise that each of them spent the ensuing night wrapped around his favorite bedpost.

With Barker's book we come to the end of the list of those on angling that, so far as we know, were available to Walton. Whether he read them or not is, in some cases, doubtful. How much from any of them he used in *The Compleat Angler* is to a large extent conjecture. We have, as previously stated, reason to believe that he may not have been familiar with Dame Juliana's *Treatyse* at first hand and we have purposely omitted mention of John Taverner's *Certaine Experiments Concerning Fish and Fruite* (1600) since, had this important volume come into Walton's hands, it would have saved him from several errors about pike, for instance, and the breeding of eels. Doubtless there were other early anglers whose knowledge Walton shared; if they were authors, their writings have disappeared.

In the late summer of 1954, while engaged in the never-ending search among London's booksellers for rarities in the field of fresh-water angling, the present writer was offered a dilapidated little volume from the press, in 1577, of the well-known printer Henry Middleton. It retains what appears to be its original vellum binding, the inside covers faced with part sheets from an earlier rubricated manuscript. The dealer had gotten it through a local "picker" in a package of odds and ends from the attic of a country house. Beyond this it had no provenance except what we learn from certain inscriptions penned by previous owners:

Robert Stapleton His Booke Anno Domini 1646.

Thomas Dale His Fishing Booke Anno Dom. 88 (i.e. 1788?)

Eli Baker's Fishing Book Stoke on trent Staffordshire Septr. 1841.

The bookseller had lent his find to the British Museum hoping that, despite its mutilated condition (several pages missing, including the title-page), the Museum's experts might, from internal evidence, identify the author. Mr. D. E. Rhodes of the British Museum examined the book. He published his findings among "Bibliographical Notes" in *The Library* (Fifth Series, X, No. 2 [June, 1955] 123-125) under the heading "A New

Introduction

Line for the *Angler*, 1577" and begins his contribution with the statement that "A book of 1577 which has recently come to my notice seems to be completely unrecorded: it is neither in the *S.T.C.* nor in the Stationers' Register, and it is not in the piscatorial bibliographies of Westwood and D. Mulder Bosgoed." Then follows a bibliographical description and some interesting remarks on Conrad Gesner's oft repeated story about a pike of fantastic age which appears both in our book and in Walton's. Finally, Mr. Rhodes brings up the question "whether or not *The Arte of Angling* printed by Henry Middleton in 1577 was known to Walton and used by him as a source-book."

This is for the reader to decide, but the present writer thought so well of the possibility and of the importance of the only English book on angling known to have been put into print between Dame Juliana's of 1496 and Mascall's of 1590, that he presented this unique copy to the Princeton University Library, to be reissued in facsimile, together with a reprint in more modern English —for easier reading.

The unknown author of *The Arte of Angling* (if only we had the missing title-page with his name on it!) lived near the market town of Saint Ives ("three mile from us by land and four good mile by water") in Huntingdonshire. He fished "our river Ouse" and tells of a bream taken with a net "in drawing the water at Huntingdon bridge"—a very ancient bridge built in the fourteenth century and still standing. We may guess that he was married and that his wife was

[7]

not sympathetic toward angling as a husband's pastime, though, when it came to cooking her man's catch, she was an artist with pots and pans. Our author was a conservationist and, from the instructions he gave his pupil, we may be certain that he was a thoughtful and practiced member of the brotherhood. Unfortunately, he stops short of giving information on trout fishing. "I dare not well deal in the angling of the trout, for displeasing of one of our wardens, which either is counted the best trouter in England, or so thinketh, who would not (as I suppose) have the taking of that fish common." No harm can come of trying to guess what this means. There are many kinds of wardens. If this particularly fearsome individual was interested in the protection of privately owned trout waters and Mr. X (our author) was under obligation to him for such favor as a day's fishing now and then, and if the "warden" was opposed to the appearance in print of anything that might promote the success of local poachers, the reason for Mr. X's reticence is clear enough. Perhaps he did write about trout fishing at some later date, for he promises that he "will speak of those and other in my next aditiō." What became of the aditiō, if it was ever written?

The feminine role in *The Arte* is played by Piscator's wife Cisley (Cecilia) who voices a low opinion of angling, an unhealthy sport capable of producing husbands under foot: "I would he had neuer knowen what angling ment. I thinke he had neuer known what the colicke had ment, if he had not known what angling had ment. . . .

Introduction

Surely I suppose so, with his long standing, long fasting, & coldenesse of his feete, yea and sometimes sitting on the cold ground: for all is one to him, whether he catch or not catch: yea and sometimes he cōmeth home with the collick in deed, and is not wel of two or three dayes after, so that I hope he will giue it ouer shortly." Cisley appears to have been the first English-speaking damsel to get her complaint against a pastime that she does not share with the man of the house placed upon the printed page. She is far from being the last!

It is interesting to note that *The Arte of Angling* does not follow the normal sequence of what we have called the "Berners pattern," though all the elements of the pattern are present. Instead of beginning with angling as the best of sports, followed by instructions for its practice and enjoyment and ending with a portrayal of the ideal angler, the *Arte* opens with a fishing scene (a pupil is being instructed), then wanders in and out of the pattern without regard to standard sequence. In its disorderly way this all adds up, with important variations, to what we have in others (Berners to Walton and beyond):

1) *The Arte* proclaims angling an excellent sport but does *not* compare it with other sports to their disparagement.
2) It gives detailed instructions on how to catch certain fishes—tackle, baits, tactics.
3) It enumerates the virtues of the perfect angler, no less than thirteen of them— faith, hope, love, patience, humility, forti-

tude, knowledge, liberality, contentment with negative results, piety (the use of prayer), ability to go uncomplainingly without food, charity (giving fish to the needy) and memory (don't leave any of your kit behind when you start nor when you return home).

Truly Saint Piscator in the flesh!

Our author's ethics, morals, and piety are beyond praise; in fact, he may well have been a nonconformist clergyman who had traveled abroad ("when I dwelt in Savoye"). His literary style is on the stilted side; a blunt and practical person, his dialogue is built on brief questions and pointed answers—few flights of fancy. Quite different from Walton, who loves lengthy digressions and, as he ages (fourth and fifth editions), becomes quite garrulous. Our unknown is a lover of nature and, within reason, of his fellow man but cannot express himself with the easy flow of language and the beauty of ideas that adorn *The Compleat Angler*.

Returning to Mr. Rhodes' question "whether or not *The Arte of Angling* . . . was known to Walton and used by him as a source-book" (a question to which no definite answer can be given) we are, nevertheless, in a fairly strong position if we assume that it was known to Walton and that he made some use of it. A startling bit of evidence is presented in the heading of the first page—"A Dialogue betweene Viator and Piscator." Dialogue is, to be sure, one of the earliest literary forms. But we have no record of its use in a book on angling until Walton invented (?) Piscator and Viator (the latter becomes Venator in the second and later editions), the same two whose conversations are set forth in *The Arte of Angling.* Why did Walton drop Viator? Can he have regretted following *The Arte* in this respect too closely?

The author of *The Arte* was misinformed, as was Walton, on certain matters of historic fact. He tells us the carp is "a fish not long knowen in England." Walton says "nor hath been long in England" and gives Mascall credit for having introduced it into English waters. Either they were neither of them familiar with Dame Juliana Berners' *Treatyse* or had read it inattentatively. She tells us: "The carp is a deyntous fysshe; but there ben but fewe in England. And therefore I wryte the lasse of hym. He is an euyll fysshe to take." By whom was Walton led astray?

It is easy enough to quote *The Arte* as giving information also supplied by Walton—the proper way, for instance, to bait one's hook with a dead minnow, the habits and peculiarities of certain fishes, and the best way to prepare them for the table, the relative importance of the skills a beginner must learn. As anglers the two men have so much in common as to methods, tactics, etc., that the present writer is willing to record, with a becoming amount of hesitation, his belief that in *The Arte of Angling* we do have a source book for *The Compleat Angler.* If others do not agree, so much the better, for what can be more delightful than one's fireside of a winter's evening with some favorite companion of the summer's

The Arte of Angling

holiday—just arguing in solid comfort and occasionally refilling an empty glass. To agree before bedtime is fatal.

By now you have been introduced, however imperfectly, gentle Lector, to *The Arte of Angling*, and it is time to begin "A Dialogue between Viator and Piscator," which is the meat of the matter. But before one sits down to piscatorial meat it is proper to express an angler's thanks, and what more graceful grace can one offer than that of the author of our little book:

"Almightie God, that these did make,
  As saith his holy book:
And gaue me cunning them to take,
  And brought them to my hooke.
To him be praise for euermore,
  That daily doth vs feede:
And doth increase by spaun such store,
  To serue vs at our neede."

CARL OTTO V. KIENBUSCH

[12]

The Arte of Angling

Modernized Text

The modernized text of *The Arte of Angling* which follows has been prepared for the convenience of readers who find black letter a strain and Elizabethan spelling and punctuation confusing. All capitalization, punctuation, and spelling of the original have been changed to modern forms, and antiquated grammar has been altered. Completely obsolete words are followed by their modern equivalents within square brackets in the text when a word or two will suffice. More complicated meanings and references have been relegated to the notes. In the margins the signatures of the pages of the original have been added for ready reference to the facsimile.

The first draft of this modern transcription was prepared by Mr. Lucien Bergeron.

❖

The explanatory notes have been prepared by Dr. Henry L. Savage, Archivist in the Princeton University Library, with a few additions and revisions by the General Editor. For expert zoological advice on insects, earthworms, and other invertebrates, Dr. Savage is grateful to Mr. John C. Pallister, Research Associate on Insects at the American Museum of Natural History, and, particularly, to Mr. Harry B. Weiss, Director Emeritus of Plant Industry, Department of Agriculture of the State of New Jersey; for other assistance to Dr. Clyde Hamilton of Rutgers University and Mr. James Clark, Department of Grounds and Buildings, Princeton University.

References to *The Compleat Angler* are to the edition of Edward Jesse, London, 1896.

A Dialogue between Viator and Piscator

A

[VIATOR.] What, friend Piscator, are you even at it so early?

PISCATOR. Yea, the proverb is truly in me verified: early up and never the near;[1] all the speed is in the morning.

VI. Is it even so? May I be so bold as to look into your pail?

PI. Yea, hardily [by all means].

VI. Why, here is nothing, not one fin!

PI. No, not one eye, truly.

VI. But, I pray you, how long have you been here?

PI. I have been here this hour and have not had one bite.

VI. How cometh that to pass?

PI. Well enough.

VI. Nay, you should say ill enough, for if I [A^v] should rise so early and in such a whistling cold morning, and stand an hour by the waterside with mine angle[2] and catch not a fish, no, nor have so much as one bite, they should bite on the

---

[1] *early up and never the near*: i.e., though rising early, none the nearer to success. A well-known proverb, quoted by the dramatists Greene, Field, Webster, and Jonson. See M. Tilley, *Dictionary of Proverbs in England*, Ann Arbor, 1950, E 27.

Proverbs are hereafter cited under the name Tilley and the numeration he employs.

[2] *angle*: fishing rod.

bridle³ for one of us. I would give them the bag⁴
and bid them adieu, and also make my reckoning
that it had been ill enough with me, as I said,
and not well enough.

Pɪ. Yea, sir. When I said well enough, I did
not mean of my not taking of fish, but that it
might well enough be, by a reason two or three,
to render the cause or causes of their not biting.

Vɪ. And do you intend to tarry until those
causes be over?

Pɪ. I will not say so. But I intend to try one
hour longer, by God's grace, and then if they bite
not, farewell they.

Aᵢᵢ Vɪ. Say you so? May a man take a stool and sit
down on the ground by you until that hour be
over?

Pɪ. Yea, so that you sit not over near the water.

Vɪ. Nay, I trow, I will sit far enough off for
[to avoid] slipping in.

Pɪ. I do not mean therefor,⁵ but I would not
have you sit so that the fish may see either your
shadow, your face, or any part of you.

Vɪ. And why? Are they so quick of sight?

Pɪ. Look, what they lack in hearing, it is supplied unto them in seeing chiefly, and also in feeling and tasting; therefore with the least moving
they shun straight, unless it be the pickerel.

Vɪ. Well, now I am set, may I then talk and
not hinder your fishing?

³ *bite on the bridle*: vex themselves but get no amends.
Tilley B 670.

⁴ *give them the bag*: leave them in the lurch. Tilley
B 32.

⁵ *therefor*: i.e., not for the reason you think.

P<small>I</small>. Spare not, but not too loud!

V<small>I</small>. Do the fish then hear? [A<small>II</small>ᵛ]

P<small>I</small>. No, you may talk, whoop, or hallo and never stir them, but I would not gladly by your loud talking that either some bungler, idle person, or jester might thereby resort unto us; and also I know not what you have to say, for friends, as they seldom meet, so spare they not to utter secrets which loud talk doth oftentimes hurt; and the truth is, the water hath an echo more than the land, and therefore easlier heard. Now, what have you to say?

V<small>I</small>. Oh, there was a bite!

P<small>I</small>. Yea, and a hit [strike].

V<small>I</small>. Why, have you her?

P<small>I</small>. Nay, not yet, but I hope to have. Lo, how say you? Now I have her indeed!

V<small>I</small>. Surely well said. Now of like [probably], the sport doth begin. Oh, cast in again for another.

P<small>I</small>. So will I, and doubt you not, my friend A<small>III</small> Viator, but you shall see sport.

V<small>I</small>. How know you?

P<small>I</small>. Nay, soft there, but tell me anon whether I said true or no. Now a [in] God's name, have among them! You shall see another bite straightway, and mark when my float is in the same place that I had my last bite in.

V<small>I</small>. Why?

P<small>I</small>. There shall you see the bite again.

V<small>I</small>. Now it is at the place almost. Now there is a bite, indeed! Well struck! Ye have her again.

[17]

Pi. I shall have by and by,[6] I hope.

Vi. Up with her, man!

Pi. No haste, but good;[7] it is a good fish.

Vi. Therefore if your angle were in my hand, I would make the more haste and toss her up over my head.

Pi. Haste, indeed, might so make waste.[8] Lo, here she is now!

[A_iii^v]   Vi. Surely it is a trim fish. I pray you, lay in again, for I see now here will be sport indeed.

Pi. I will. I have spied a fault which I had need to mend, but you are so hasty.

Vi. Tush! Mend your faults soon as most do,[9] and ply your sport. So lo, now another bite by and by, I warrant you.

Pi. I hope so.

Vi. Strike!

Pi. I warrant you, let me alone. If I miss a bite, tell me.[10]

Vi. You have her again.

Pi. God send her me, for it is a good fish, and a dace, I believe.

Vi. Why, what are the other two?

---

6 *by and by*: immediately. Cf. Matt. 13:21: "When tribulation or persecution ariseth because of the word, by and by he is offended."

7 *No haste, but good*: Tilley H 199: "It is a saynge that an yll haste is not good."

8 *Haste, indeed, might so make waste*: Tilley H 189: "But the old saying is, haste makethe waste."

9 *Mend your faults soon as most do*: never mind the fault. Tilley F 103: "It is more easie to finde a fault then to amend it."

10 *If I miss a bite, tell me*: sarcasm.

Pɪ. Roaches.

Vɪ. Can you tell before you see her what kind of fish it is?

Pɪ. I have a guess. I told you it was a dace.

Vɪ. Indeed, now you have her. Your guess was A₁₁₁₁ a true guess, belike, and I must needs say it is another kind, I see by her making and color, for she is rounder and whiter. How now! Why lay you not in again?

Pɪ. Nay, now I will sit down by you awhile and mend a fault.

Vɪ. I pray you, cast in once more for my pleasure.

Pɪ. What and I lose my hook?

Vɪ. Farewell it; there is but a hook lost.

Pɪ. Yea, friend, a good hook is not so soon found again. But to pleasure you, there it is, and you shall see me lose it straight.

Vɪ. I warrant you for an egg at Easter.[11]

Pɪ. Your warrant is as good as an obligation sealed with butter.[12]

Vɪ. There was a fair bite.

Pɪ. You say true, and a foul hit, for all is lost. [A₁₁₁₁ᵛ] Thus it is to be ruled by you. It is [a] marvel if all be not gone. I had warning; I might have taken heed. There is a hook gone; now I must sit down with loss.

Vɪ. I am sorry now that you sat not down afore. Have you any more hooks here?

[11] *I warrant you for an egg at Easter*: Tilley E 75: "The English Tradition was, Hai for an Egg at Easter."
[12] *sealed with butter*: i.e., worthless. Tilley B 769.

Pı. Yea, I trow, or else I were but a simple fisher. If I had not store of hooks about me, I might put up pipes.[13]

Vı. How will you do to set it on? Have you any thread about you?

Pı. You are a wise man! Do you think that anglers do use to set on their hooks with thread?

Vı. Why not, and make a hook of a bowed pin and an angle of a stick?

Pı. Like workman, like tool![14] You speak according to your knowledge. I would you had such an angle here, that you might try your cunning whilst I were setting on of my hook.

Vı. So would I. I would pull them up, I trow.

Pı. Or else you cannot tell. What bait would ye have?

Vı. One of yours.

Pı. You should pardon me.

Vı. Then I would dig up a worm with my knife hereabouts and put it on.

Pı. And how would you do for a float?

Vı. Tush! When I felt the fish bite, then I would pull and throw her up, or else I would tie a little rotten stick about my line. Laugh you?

Pı. Why, you would make a sick man to laugh.

Vı. Now, surely, lend me but a fathom of thread, and you shall see me an angler straight.

Pı. What, so soon?

[A$_v^v$] Vı. Yea, for I have a pin, and I will cut a wand out of this willow hereby, and dig up a worm, as

A$_v$

13 *I might put up pipes*: shut up shop; quit. Tilley P 345.
14 *Like workman, like tool*: A variant of the proverb "The workman is known by his work" (Tilley W 860) or "A workman is known by his tools."

I said, if you will not lend me a bait, and catch some or ever you be ready, you sit so long fiddling about tying on of your hook.

Pi. So then you would have your rod, your line, your hook, your bait, and your fish or ever I were ready to lay in again. But, good sir, where be your plummets[15] and your plumb?[16]

Vi. Nay, then we shall never have done: the bait will sink of itself with the weight of the pin, and as for the plumb, I cannot tell what it means.

Pi. I think so, nor shall not at my hand. And where is your meat?

Vi. Meat, quoth ye? They shall be my meat when I have catched them.

Pi. Well said. That was well put to.[17]

Vi. Say you so? Up I will for it and prepare myself.

Pi. Tush, tush! I pray you sit still, for now you [A_{vi}] do no harm. You were as good sit still for naught as rise for naught. I took loss even now at your request. Either take ye no harm or do none at my request.

Vi. Now you make me to laugh. You are afraid that I should kill them up before you be ready.

Pi. If you had already that you speak of, where is the beard [barb] of your hook?

---

15 *plummets*: "In angling, a small piece of lead attached to a fishing-line, as a weight to keep the float in an upright position; as an anchor in ledgar fishing." (NED, *plummet*, sb., 5.c.) "Ledgar fishing" occurs when the angler's bait, hook, and line are made to remain in one place, i.e., by the plummet.

16 *plumb*: "A plummet used by anglers to measure the depth of a stream or pond." (NED. sb. 1.b.)

17 *well put to*: well set about. (NED. sb. 51.b.)

Vi. I tell you they should never have leisure to slip off, I would so fling them to land.

Pi. Why, is there no more use to the beard belonging but to hold on the fish?

Vi. Not that I know. Is there?

Pi. Nay, soft. You came not where it grew.[18] You speak, indeed, according to your knowledge. Now I am ready.

[A$_{vi}$^{v}] Vi. It is time, I trow. I pray you, let me see how you have tied it on.

Pi. Tied it on?[19] How rightly you have your terms!

Vi. How then! Bound it on?

Pi. Even which you will.

Vi. Oh, so fine you be! There is no occupation, I perceive, but there is a glory in it.

Pi. So, so. It will be a good while or ever you be a good fisher.

Vi. Why?

Pi. You do but jest at it, and therefore I see well that you mind not to learn to angle.

Vi. Yes, truly, of all crafts I would most gladly have it taught me but for one thing, and that is I love not to stand, as I perceive that you do, sometimes an whole hour and take not a fish; for they must bite straightway with me, or I am

18 *You came not where it grew*: a play on the word "beard."

19 *Tied it on*: Needless to say, the hook is not tied on or bound on to the line. It is attached by a running knot to a cast or collar of horsehair, which is in turn attached to the end of the running line. Sixteenth-century lines were made of horsehair. They could be strengthened by the interweaving of several hairs and tapered off to take the hook.

gone; for who would stand gazing on the water so long and have no sport? It is but tedious idle- [A$_{vii}$] ness, yea, and sometimes a wet skin; yea, head and all, if his foot slip. And in a cold morning he may catch that in his feet that will not out of his head a good while after, and I think it is not very good for the colic.

P$_I$. Then it is well that ye know no more of it, seeing that you can tell of so many discommodities that doth belong unto it; but what if a man can tell you how not only to avoid all these but also to have twice so many commodities [benefits] by it, if he once know the art thoroughly?

V$_I$. There are my forenamed two terms mended.[20] I see well that angling is neither an occupation nor a craft but an art, and not without some skill. For I do, indeed, suppose that he which maketh an occupation of it may often eat his bread dry, yea, and perhaps bring him to beg it; but I do think that you do use it in the best [A$_{vii}$^{v}] kind, and that is for recreation, for pastime, and sometimes to get you a stomach.[21]

P$_I$. It may be used of sundry men to sundry ends, and of the cunning man to all those ends that are lawful.

V$_I$. But how now, all this while and not a fish? This I like not. The bite is done. I thought you tarried too long or ever you threw in your bait again, or else my talk, though as you say that it trouble not the fish, yet it may be that it hath troubled you, so that you tend not so well

---

[20] *forenamed two terms mended*: i.e., there the terms used, craft and occupation, are corrected.

[21] *get you a stomach*: give you an appetite.

to your fishing as you did before you were moved.

Pɪ. Indeed, I could be well content to have less talk now, my mess of fish being so little that I might the more attentively take heed; for I [Aᵥᵢᵢᵢ] have lost a bite or two that you saw not and some that I did not see, nor you neither, until it was past, besides some practices that belong to this science that now I would put in use, if you were not here, to make up my dish of fish withal or ever I went, or else it should go hard.

Vɪ. Why then I perceive I am now a let [hindrance] unto you. But I hope you be not angry, for surely I meant nothing but mirth. Notwithstanding, I will trouble you no longer, but leave you where I found you; and St. Peter's Master²² be with you, praying you not to be offended, for I perceive the fisherman may sometimes be displeased, as well as hawkers or hunters.

Pɪ. Nay, truly, but I must needs tell you that we be not altogether void of passions and choler. Yet assure yourself, as you came my friend, so [Aᵥᵢᵢᵢᵛ] shall you go on my behalf; and that shall ye well know if you will come to me soon to supper. And then shall ye be a partaker, not only at my table of my day's work, but also, if you entreat me fair and bring a quart of sack with you and mind [wish], indeed, to be acquainted in our ministry and to know the mysteries of it, you shall be welcome, and I pray you come.

²² *St. Peter's Master*: Christ. Peter is, of course, patron of fishermen. Cf. the motto on the title-page of the first edition of *The Compleat Angler*, "Simon Peter said, I go a fishing: and they said, We also will go with thee." John 21:3. Correctly quoted in the second edition.

Vɪ. I thank you. I will not fail, God willing. God be with you until soon. Now use your knacks,[23] for I am gone.

Pɪ. Come again, I pray you, and help me with your hand a little, for I have now need of your help. I have struck [hooked] a good fish and shall not, I fear me, be able to land her alone.

Vɪ. It is a great one, indeed, by the bending of your angle. What fish is it, trow you?

Pɪ. A perch it should be, by the grossness of the bite and by the hardness of the strike and his B shattering.[24]

Vɪ. Give me your angle and take you him up when he comes to the bankside.

Pɪ. Nay, not so, for so we might lose him, for the guiding of the line is one of the best feats when a good fish is struck. It is a perch, indeed, and that a fair one. God send us well to land him; he will mend our dish well. See how he gapes, stares, and holds up his bristles.[25] I must pray you to lie down flat on your belly and hold fast by the ground with your one hand, or else let me tread on the skirts of your coat with my left foot that you slip not in, and take him up with your

23 *knacks*: tricks, devices, artifices.

24 *shattering*: shaking, waving, moving to and fro. (NED, *shatter*, v.6.)

25 *holds up his bristles*: The perch's "front dorsal has from 13 or 14 sharp spinous rays: a weapon of defence and offence, as some anglers have discovered when they have incautiously handled the fish. . . . He is a plucky fighter . . . when he sallies forth from his concealment, with his spiny gillcovers distended and prickly dorsal fin erect." (A. Jardine, *Pike and Perch*, Anglers' Library, London, 1898, pp. 145-6.)

other hand; for I will with my line lead him hard [securely] to the bank, for now he is tired.

Vɪ. Yea, but how shall I deal with him for his pricks, for he hath more than you see?

[Bᵛ] Pɪ. Put your finger under his throat, under one of his gills, into his mouth. I mean your fore-finger, and your thumb into his mouth, and so your finger and your thumb, meeting in his mouth, hold them fast together, and so throw him up lustily to land, for that line and those hooks will not break.

Vɪ. He will bite me.

Pɪ. No, I warrant you, do as I bid you. He hath no teeth in his mouth,²⁶ they be down in his throat.

Vɪ. How shall we now do? He holdeth his chaps together as hard as may be.

Pɪ. Take him hard by the nape of the neck and so bring him up.

Vɪ. I will. I have him now.

Pɪ. Hold fast whilst I lay down mine angle and help you up, because you have but one hand. So, well said. Now we have him.

B₁₁ Vɪ. Surely, surely, it is a good fish. How would you have done if I had not been here? I perceive now that it is meet for you to have one with you. What have we there? What, but one hair?²⁷ Why that passeth [description]!

²⁶ *He hath no teeth in his mouth*: Walton says other-wise, p. 230: "He . . . carries his teeth in his mouth, which is very large."

²⁷ *one hair*: one horsehair. The perch, "a bold biter," has severed all the strands of the horsehair line but one.

PI. No, indeed, for I came today to this plat[28] a-roaching and therefore brought but my roach gear and, like a wise man, left one of my tools at home for haste, which if I had brought, I could have landed him without your help.

VI. I pray you, be not without your shift [excuse], and all to drive me away. Well, fare you well now, indeed.

PI. God be with you, and I thank you for your pains.

PISCATOR AND HIS WIFE, CISLEY

[PI.] How now, wife, is the broth ready?

CI. Indeed, I have had good leisure! Good [B] Lord, husband, where have you been all this day? Have you dined?

PI. No, truly. My first bread is yet to eat since you saw me, therefore let my supper be ready as soon as may be.

CI. So will I, but what have you brought?

PI. Fetch me a platter and you shall see.

CI. Here is one. Shall I take them out?

PI. No, dame, I will take them out and lay every sort by themselves. How say you, Cisley, is there not a good dish?

CI. I am glad now that I did throw an old shoe[29] after you in the morning. Here is a mess[30] indeed.

28 *plat*: locality, spot of ground. (NED, *plat*, sb2 II 8b.)
29 *throw an old shoe*: as an augury of good luck. See Tilley, S 372.
30 *mess*: a quantity of meat sufficient to make a dish. (NED, *mess*, sb. 1.c.) "Mess of fish" is now an Americanism. (NED, sb. 1.d.)

Pɪ. Your old shoe was fit for an old foolish woman to have thrown, that hath more confi-
B_iii dence in such dismal toys than in the providence of God Who guideth as well the fishes in the sea as the fowls in the air. But I know you speak merrily, as I did when I bade you do it.

Cɪ. How will you have them dressed? For, as here be many sorts, so may you have them dressed after sundry manners.

Pɪ. Let them, I pray you, be ordered after the best manner, for my friend Viator will be here at supper.

Cɪ. They shall.

Vɪᴀᴛᴏʀ. Ho, God be here.

Pɪ. Oh, are you come? Come near, I know you by your voice.

Vɪ. Ah, you are come home, I perceive.

Pɪ. Now surely you are welcome. What, and your sack too! That is honestly said. Is it good sack?

[B_iii^v] Vɪ. I cannot tell, for of all wines I love it not. Therefore I did not say [essay, try].

Pɪ. And why? Do you know anything by [about] it?

Vɪ. Yea, Piscator, I have seen such lively fellows—short with sharp heads, as they say that sometimes you fish withal—poured out into a goblet; for when the wine hath been drunk, there have they lain.[31]

31 *lively fellows . . . have they lain*: the reference is to the larvae of *Drosophilae*, fruit or vinegar flies. The adult flies are plainly visible, and their larvae or maggots are also. "The adults could lay their eggs around the edges

Pɪ. Tush! If you will neither eat nor drink of anything that quick cattle[32] is in or will breed in, you will hardly hold them in your mouth while you angle, that they may be the readier to put on your hook.

Vɪ. Out upon it, and if I wist that that were of necessity, I would either angle in those months when they be out of season or else with some other baits as good, or not at all.

Pɪ. Well, sit down, I pray you. Our supper will come in by and by. We will have one fit [spell] B_{iiii} at fishing until meat come.

Vɪ. Why then, I pray you, let us know somewhat of the antiquity of it.

Pɪ. Nay, let me rather make mine introduction to the matter and so come to that afterward. First, you must understand that, as God did make all things for man, so should he have had a great deal of more commodious pleasure in his creatures than he hath, had he not by his disobedience made them both disobedient and hurtful. Yea, I do suppose that neither the heavens or any powers above, neither the earth or anything therein, either could or would have hurt man, if man had not first hurt himself. And also the huge sea, with all the benefits thereof, and all others of waters, as meres, lakes, ponds, rivers, and streams, should have given their goods and [B_{iiii}^v]

---

of casks of fermented sack and soon there would be maggots in the sack and they would have pointed heads that could readily be seen and they would also be lively." Information from H. B. Weiss, personal letter, 5-12-56.

[32] *quick cattle*: live insects. Cattle is here a collective noun. (NED, sb. ɪɪ.7.)

riches unto man if man had not given himself to sin and so to Satan. By which means he hath not only lost, as I said, and so all we that come of him, infinite commodities, but also those that he hath he must win them with great care and sore labor and with all device, policy, and art that he can, sometimes not without the peril of his life. For there is not the smallest fish that is, that is not now too good for a man (having stream at will),³³ without his great industry to catch her.

Vi. Why then, if earthly things are so hard to come by, by reason of our former father's fall, how are we able to come by heavenly things that are beyond our labor? I suppose that we are far weaker that way.

B᷎ Pi. It is true. For He that said *In sudore vultus tui, etc.*³⁴ (in the sweat of thy brows thou shalt get thy living, and that the earth should bear naught but brambles and briars, and that, as man came from earth, so to earth he should return) did not say that man in his labors should get heaven; but only the winning of heaven He left to One that never fell and so by Him to have it, and all other good things also—Christ Jesus, I mean.

Vi. Well, now to your matter again.

Pi. To return yet, for all that, the same Almighty God hath not so avenged the fall and offence of man that he should be altogether over pressed with careful travail, but hath spiced man's pains with delight, pastime, and recreation, many

³³ *having stream at will*: the fish having the free run of the stream.
³⁴ *In sudore, etc.*: quotation from Genesis: 3:19.

ways: in the finding, winning, or ending of his labors, whereof the fisher, falconer, and hunter [B$_v^v$] are well able to report. And, as the same Almighty hath not made all kind of living creatures upon earth to be but one, but divided them into beasts, fowls, fishes, and worms [reptiles], and they of diverse sorts in every kind, so hath he given to sundry men, sundry minds; some in this, and some in that to have pleasure. For if all his living creatures should have been of one sort, as all fishes, all beasts, or all fowls, so had loathsomeness and waste hurt appetite and pleasure. But now to speak more particularly and to our purpose. As in fishing, fowling, and hunting there is degrees both of costs, pains, pleasures, and profits, so what cost, pain, pleasure, or profit the hunter or hawker hath, as I am not skillful in either of them, so do I leave such as would know to the sundry books set out by sundry men [B$_{vi}$] and in sundry tongues that doth write of them both at large. Neither do I purpose so to speak unto you of fishing as severally to tell of all the cost, pain, pleasure, or profit that is in that marvelous and wonderful science.

Vi. No, friend Piscator, I come not therefor; only, I pray you, speak of angling.

Pi. So I will, as of that pleasure that I have always most recreated myself withal, and had most delight in, and is most meetest for a solitary man, and is also of light cost. Yet do I not intend to make myself so skillful unto you in the art of angling as to leave out nothing that might be said, no more than you shall find me to contemn that which hath been put in print heretofore.

[B_{vi}^v] For this I know: that both time, place, kind [nature], and custom is not so known unto me but that I may want in any of the four, yea, and in all, to say that may be said. But what I do know by report, by reading, or by experience, by myself at home or abroad, I will, God willing, not hide it from you; and if you can learn more of any others, or that at this time I shall forget or hereafter find any more knowledge, take that for advantage. And this I tell you plain: that the covetous and greedy man (for avoiding spoil)[35] may not be allowed in this fellowship; neither may the sluggard sleepy sloven be seen in this science; neither the poor man, lest it make him poorer and beg his bread to his fish; the angry man, also, and the fearful man, with the busybody, must tarry at home, and rather hunt or hawk.

VI. Why then, I pray you, what gifts must he [B_{vii}] have that shall be of your company?

PI. 1. He must have faith, believing that there is fish where he cometh to angle. 2. He must have hope that they will bite. 3. Love to the owner of the game.[36] 4. Also patience, if they will not bite, or any mishap come by losing of the fish, hook, or otherwise. 5. Humility to stoop, if need be to kneel or lie down on his belly, as you did today. 6. Fortitude, with manly courage, to deal with the biggest that cometh. 7. Knowledge adjoined to wisdom, to devise all manner of ways how to

35 *for avoiding spoil*: in order to avoid despoliation, the behavior of a game-hog.
36 *Love to the owner of the game*: he must be no poacher.

[32]

make them bite and to find the fault. 8. Liberality in feeding of them. 9. A content mind with a sufficient mess, yea, and though you go home without. 10. Also he must use prayer, knowing that it is God that doth bring both fowl to the net and fish to the bait. 11. Fasting he may not be offended withal, but acquaint himself with it, if [B_{vii}^v] it be from morning until night, to abide and seek for the bite. 12. Also he must do alms deeds; that is to say, if he meet a sickly poor body or doth know any such in the parish that would be glad of a few fishes to make a little broth withal (as often times is desired of sick persons), then he may not stick to send them some or altogether.[37] And if he have none, yet with all diligence that may [be, he][38] try with his angle to get some for the diseased person. 13. The last point of all the inward gifts that doth belong to an angler, is memory, that is, that he forget nothing at home when he setteth out, nor anything behind him at his return.[39]

[37] *altogether*: the whole catch.
[38] [*be, he*]: the reading is conjectural. The paper has been worn away at this point.
[39] This list of the thirteen inward gifts of the angler is an interesting parody or humorous approximation of the catalogues of Christian virtues so popular in the time. The first three, faith, hope, and charity (or love), are the first of the cardinal virtues. Most of the others—knowledge, liberality, fortitude, fasting, etc.—belong in one or another of the familiar lists of qualities desirable for Christians, but the list is not a precise parody of any of the standard Christian ones.

This list of Piscator's was evidently familiar to seventeenth-century writers on angling. John Dennys in his *The Secrets of Angling*, 1613, follows it item for item

Vi. Why, man, if he have an angle and baits, what need any more? And a small memory will serve for those two.

[TWO PAGES OF THE BOOK ARE MISSING HERE. WHEN THE TEXT RESUMES, PISCATOR IS GIVING DIRECTIONS FOR MAKING A CERTAIN KIND OF FLOAT.]

C   Pi. You must take two swan's quills—one quill must be greater than another—and cut off both the stopped ends, and then put the one cut end into the other as hard as you can for cleaving of the uttermost, that they may be close for taking of water. And look that they have no holes in the smaller ends, and that quill that is within the other, let that be lowest in the water. Then must you take another swan's quill and cut it in two such pieces as may be put on each end of your float one, so that the ends of your double quill, or float, appear out when your line is put through those two pieces; as for example, here is one ready-made.

Here must we stay. Now is supper come.

[Cᵛ]   Vi. I am the more sorry, for your talk is meat and drink to me.³⁹ᵃ

Pi. Yea, but meat and drink is fitter for me that have not eaten today. Well, let us have grace.

---

except that he inverts 7 and 8 and omits 12. Markham in his *Art of Angling*, 1614, says, "Now for the inward qualities of the minde, albeit some Writers reduce them to twelve heads . . . yet I must draw them into many branches." (1660 ed., pp. 59-60.) But later (pp. 60-62) he repeats Piscator's list slightly reordered, with prudence and thankfulness substituted for prayer and knowledge.

³⁹ᵃ *is meat and drink to me*: proverbial. See Tilley M 842.

Vi. Have ye not a fish grace?

Pi. Yes, that I have, and that for an angler.

Almighty God, that these did make,
  As saith his holy book,
And gave me cunning them to take,
  And brought them to my hook;
To him be praise for evermore,
  That daily doth us feed,
And doth increase by spawn such store
  To serve us at our need.

Vi. A very good grace, and a fit. Now, I pray you, let your Cisley come in.

Pi. Call your mother in, maid.

Vi. What fish call you these?

Pi. Gudgeons.

Vi. They be very good, indeed, well dressed. C$_{ii}$ How take you these?

Pi. These are as fit for a young beginner[40] as may be, for one bait doth serve them at all seasons, and you may make them to bite all day if you have sundry places. Come, wife, come! Thou thinkest that nothing is well done unless thou be at the one end of it. Sit down and eat, for I am hungry.

Ci. I believe [it] well. How like you your broth?

Pi. Hunger findeth no fault.[40a]

[40] *beginner*: cf. Walton, p. 257: "he is an excellent fish to enter a young angler, being easy to be taken with a small red-worm." And John Dennys says, "This fish the fittest for a learner is." (*The Secrets of Angling*, Westwood ed., 1883, p. 41.)

[40a] *Hunger findeth no fault*: proverbial. See Tilley H 814.

VI. But, I pray you, teach me to kill these pleasant fishes.

CI. I pray you, sir, let my husband awhile alone until he have eaten, and then you cannot please him better at meat than to talk of angling, though for my part I would he had never known what angling meant.

VI. Why, I pray you?

[C₁₁ᵛ] CI. I think he had never known what the colic had meant, if he had not known what angling had meant.

VI. Is it even so?

PI. Soft, dame!

VI. Nay, I pray you, let us two alone, and eat you awhile, for I believe that your wife is not fasting, no more than I. Now, mistress, is it true that your husband hath caught the colic with fishing?

CI. Surely I suppose so, with his long standing, long fasting, and coldness of his feet, yea, and sometimes sitting on the cold ground, for all is one to him, whether he catch or not catch. Yea, and sometimes he cometh home with the colic, indeed, and is not well of [for] two or three days after, so that I hope he will give it over shortly.

VI. Is this true?

PI. Yea, what then?

VI. Then I say, *Fælix quem faciunt aliena pericula cautum.*[41] Happy is he

41 *Fælix, etc.:* "Happy is he whom the dangers of others makes cautious." Quoted as a saying of Cyllenus's *Tibullus,* pub. 1493; see Sir Gurney Benham's *Book of Quotations.* new ed., London, 1948, p. 577b.

Modernized Text

stand you beneath him as the water runneth, so C_v
that you may angle in the thick water, and you
shall have trim sport. And if he that doth stir
the water have in a bag of linen some ground
malt, and now and then cast in as much as he
may hold between his three fingers where he
stirreth, that it may fall just where you angle, it
is the better. And you may put on two hooks at
this sport and so have a good mess quickly. Land
when you see the bite die, then remove to another
place, and so on, as your store of fish, plats,[42] and
speeding [success] is.

VI. Now cometh your wife again, and I shall
be shent [disgraced] for keeping you from eating.

PI. No, no, she knoweth this talk to be meat
and drink unto me. Now, wife, come and sit
down.

CI. We have brought you all.

VI. All, quoth ye? Indeed, here is store. Oh, [C_v^v]
here is the great perch that you took in the
morning. It is so, indeed. But what are these
lying about him?

PI. Ruffes.[43]

VI. What fish is it?

[42] *plats*: a flat-bottomed boat used for fishing. (NED, sb.
5.) *store of . . . plats*: supply of boats, i.e., boats moored at
different spots along the river bank.

[43] *Ruffes*: the ruffe (*acerina cernua*), or pope, is "similar
to a small perch, but the colouring and back fin are
different." (*Fine Angling for Coarse Fish*, ed. E. Parker,
The Lonsdale Library, IV, Philadelphia, n.d., pp. 159-60.)

P₁. Oh, excellent.

V₁. I pray you, how take you them?

C₁. Good sir, let him eat his meat.

P₁. My wife counteth me like the instrument of Lincolnshire.⁴⁴ But now that I have somewhat stayed my hunger, I can both eat and talk. The ruffe is the grossest at his bite of any fish that biteth, and is taken with the red worm⁴⁵ on the ground,⁴⁶ and where he lieth, there is he commonly alone. He is envious [malicious], bristled on the back as the perch, in each fin a sharp prick, his gills sharp at the end, and swalloweth the bait [Cᵥᵢ] at the first, great goggle-eyed, and cometh up very churlishly, and will hold his lips so hard together that you shall have much ado to open them, and commonly you must rend the gills asunder to get out your hook. He is full of black spots and like to rised [rancid] bacon, and therefore we call them little hogs. But surely an wholesome fish! With two hairs you may fish for him, he is so gross in his feeding and cometh not up gently. Hold you, there is one of them. Taste of him and tell me.

V₁. A very good fish.

P₁. There cannot be a better, and chiefly [especially] for a sick body. I count him better than either gudgeon or perch, for he eateth faster and pleasanter. The worm is his only bait that ever

⁴⁴ *instrument of Lincolnshire*: the bagpipe. Piscator says his wife is thinking of the proverb, "He is like a bagpipe, he never talks till his belly is full." Tilley, B 34.

⁴⁵ *red worm*: earthworm, angleworm. Perhaps dug up from a dunghill, since worms found there have a redder coloration than those dug from top-soil.

⁴⁶ *on the ground*: on or close to the bottom of the stream.

I did know. My master that taught me to angle could not abide to catch a ruffe; for if he took one, either he would remove or wind up and [C$_\text{vi}^\text{v}$] home for that time, he did know them so masterly among other fish. But for my part, I have been well content to deal with them, for this property they have, as is seen among the wicked: that though they see their fellows perish never so fast, yet will they not be warned, so that you shall have them as long as one is left, especially a little before a rain or in the bite time. And if you close some small worms in a ball of old black dung or earth, and cast it in where you angle for them, you shall have the better sport, for at that will they lie like little hogs, as is aforesaid. You so listen to my talk that you eat nothing.

C1. You men say that women be talkative, but here is such a number of words about nothing, as passeth [defies description].

P1. Why so I say, all is nothing with you and [C$_\text{vii}$] your kind unless it be about pins and laces, fringe and guards, fine linen and woolen, hats and hatbands, gloves and scarves; and yet I marvel that you should say that my talk hath been of nothing. For one part of the attire that now is of no small charge among you, we have a fish to father it called a ruffe, of whom I spake even now, unless you will have it the diminutive of a ruffian. But it may be that the name doth come from the ruffe, the fish, for surely the greater part that use the long gut gathered together of this fish, they may well be said to be in their ruff and like unto the ruffe in disdain.[47]

[47] *For one part . . . in disdain:* Piscator puns on ruff (a pleated neck piece), ruffe (the fish), and ruffian.

[39]

Vi. Well now, I pray you, to the taking of the perch.

Pi. The perch is a gross fish and easily taken. A red worm is his common bait,[48] but the quick [live] minnow is the best,[49] putting your hook through the corner of her lip, and so let her swim alive an ell in the water, with plummets to keep her down; and strike not over soon when you see the bite, but let him go as far as the length of your line, that he may swallow it, or else his mouth is so wide and so full of bones, and also he will many times gape for the nonce [purpose] and cast out hook and minnow. The minnow, the minnow also will somewhat bear off your hook, but when your fish is in his gullet, then all is safe, so that your hook bend not or your line break.

[C_{vii}^v]

Vi. I may fish with more hairs for him than one or two?[50]

[Pi.] That you may, with four or six, and a good, handsome, compassed [curved] hook. He will also in winter bite at a good gentle[51] or a ball of bread. A ravenous fish it is also, and liveth

---

[48] *A red worm is his common bait*: cf. Walton, p. 232: "he will bite . . . at . . . a worm, a minnow, or a little frog."

[49] *the quick minnow is the best*: cf. Walton, pp. 232-33: ". . . if you rove for a pearch with a minnow, then it is best to be alive, you sticking your hook through his back-fin; or a minnow with the hook in his upper lip, and letting him swim up and down, about mid-water or a little lower, and you still keeping him to about that depth by a cork, which ought not to be a very little one."

[50] *one or two*: i.e., a line plaited of more than one or two horse hairs.

[51] *gentle*: maggot; larva of the blue-bottle fly.

for the most part by eating up of his fellows, as [C_{viii}] the covetous enclosers⁵² do. And if you come to the lair of great perches, let your line be strong, for when you have struck one the residue will come and make such a stir about your line and him, with their bristles up, that they will deliver their fellow if you have not a good line and very good hold.

VI. Why, then, they be like to hogs, and both better than most men, which, seeing their neighbor in trouble, will rather help to keep him in trouble than to work to bring him out. But be these all the baits that do belong to the taking of a perch?

PI. No, he will bite very well at the red knotted worm, yea, and at a yellow frushe or frog, if it be a little one; and a small gudgeon is very good, but the great knotted red worm (well-ordered and well put on the hook, as we use to do [C_{viii}^v] for the chevin) is a special good bait.

VI. How mean you the ordering?

PI. As for that, I will tell you in the end for the ordering of all your baits.

VI. Then, I pray you, to the pickerel.

PI. The pickerel is also a fleshy fish, and liveth by ravening and eating of his fellows, and beareth the swinge [rule] of the fishes, and is called the freshwater wolf;⁵³ gross-witted; hath a weed of

⁵² *enclosers*: landowners who fenced in the common land of a parish or larger division. They were widely hated at this time.

⁵³ *freshwater wolf*: Izaak Walton says (p. 189) that "their life is maintained by the death of so many other fish ... which has made him, by some writers, to be called the tyrant of the rivers, or the fresh-water wolf."

his own which also he will feed on, called pickerel-weed.[54] He will be haltered,[55] and some men use that way very oft to kill him, for he will lie staring upon you, as the hare or lark, until you put the line with a snittle [noose] over his head, and so with a good stiff pole you may throw him to land. This way is best in standing [still] waters and pools.

D VI. This is a carterly,[56] rude way. I pray you, tell me how to kill him with an angle.

PI. He is so gross a ravener, as I said, that anything will kill him, for he will bite at a gentle, if it come in his mad head, but then your hook is gone, he will shear so with his teeth. When you fish for him, you must fish with an armed hook of three links,[57] and your line of sixteen or twenty hairs, and a good big float, a double hook, and a handsome roach or dace or frog. He will be killed with a great red worm, as I have proved.

VI. How shall I put on my roach or my frog?

PI. You must ripple [scratch] with your point of your knife overthwart the roach, under the gill, that the scales and skin may be taken away and opened; and then put in the end your arm-

54 *pickerel-weed*: a name commonly applied to a species of Potomogeton, pondweed (not the American pickerel-weed). Cf. Walton, p. 195: "His feeding is . . . sometimes a weed of his own called pickerel-weed."

55 *haltered*: caught with a noose.

56 *carterly*: like or befitting a carter, boorish, lacking in sporting etiquette.

57 *armed hook of three links*: a hook whipped round (armed) with a three-haired line. A link is one of the segments of which a hair-line is composed. (NED, *link*, sb.2 2.)

ing,[58] and so thrust it down the side of the roach [D^v] between the flesh and the skin, and let it come out at the tail of the fish, so drawing your links of arming gently until the hook be nothing seen but the bearded points under her gill, then put your line on, and let your float be of cork, and not passing an ell from your fish. This bait, after this manner, may be either [a] legger or a walker,[59] for if you either be weary, or would sit down

[58] *arming*: a three-haired line, which is carried down the side of the roach between flesh and skin and out at the fish's tail; the hairs of the arming must be drawn gently so that the barbs of the hook attached at its end on the leader are just visible below the gill. The upper portion of the arming (or leader) is then attached to the line, the cork float being not more than an ell (1¼ yards) from the bait. It cannot be ascertained whether the roach used is live or dead bait. Walton, p. 196, describes the preparation of the live bait as follows: ". . . having cut off his fin on his back, which may be done without hurting him,—you must take your knife . . . and betwixt the head and the fin on the back, cut or make an incision, or such a scar as you may put the arming wire (Walton League ed., p. 76: arming-wire = shank?) of your hook into it, with as little bruising or hurting the fish, as art and diligence will enable you to do; and so carrying your arming-wire, along his back, unto or near the tail of your fish, betwixt the skin and the body of it, draw out that wire or arming of your hook at another scar near to his tail: then tie him about it with thread, but no harder than of necessity, to prevent hurting the fish; and the better to avoid hurting the fish, some have a kind of probe to open the way, for the more easy entrance and passage of your wire or arming."

[59] *legger or a walker*: explained by Walton, p. 195: ". . . you may fish for pike, either with a ledger, or a walking bait . . . I call that a ledger-bait, which is fixed, or made to rest in one certain place when you shall be absent from it,—and I call that a walking-bait, which you take with you, and have ever in motion."

and look on a book, or mend your gears, or with another angle fish for roach or perch thereby, you may, throwing your bait as far into the water as you may with a long line, and lay down your rod on the bank. But look to the bite and be not far off, lest that either your pole or cane be pulled in with some good fish or that, when she hath struck herself (for so she will with swallowing the bait into her gullet) that she get not into the weed, as

D₁₁ among the cane roots, clotter leaves,[60] or her own weed, and then shall you never get her out without a boat and a reed hook unless the weeds be by the bankside. And then with a piece of pack-thread, tying your knife at the end of your pike angle, making it like a weed hook, you may shred the weeds under the fish, so may you come by fish and hook.

Vi. Is there any other way to fish for the pick-erel?

Pi. Yea, as I say, as by walking and fishing with a dead bait, and specially a bleak,[61] though she be a day old and laid against the sun, or carried between the crown of your head and the top of your hat to dry the sooner, three or four; and put your hook through her nose or nether lip, and so walk the river. And let it never stand still, but be moving of it up and down, and still drawing,

[D₁₁ᵛ] but not hastily; and when you see the float pulled at and sink, let him go as long as you may, for he will sometimes carry the bait overthwart his mouth a good while or ever that he will swallow it, and especially if that he have been struck at

---

60 *clotter leaves*: yellow water-lily (*nuphar lutea*) leaves.
61 *bleak*: a small European river fish (*alburnus lucidus*) of the carp family.

before and hardly escaped, and a good fish. Also the frog is a very good bait, the yellower the better; and the head of an eel, and a good big gudgeon, quick.

Cɪ. You eat no meat now; therefore it may be taken away.

Pɪ. Indeed, as you know, wife, it is better to fill my belly than mine eye[61a]; and a little thing doth suffice nature, and this talk is for my turn.

Vɪ. Well, then, if it please you, let us have a cup of sack and an apple or a pear, and then let us rise, a God's name.

Pɪ. Not so, for I love to take mine ease in mine inn,[62] and yet a bite or two more. Reach, wife, that other dish near me.

Vɪ. What fish is this, I pray you, in the midst? D_{iii}

Pɪ. It is a chub and would have been within this year a chevin.[63] Say [try], I pray you, a morsel of him. Those that lie about him are roaches.

Vɪ. It is a sweet fish, but he eateth somewhat flashly [insipidly] and is full of bones.

Cɪ. Indeed, sir, ye say true, and therefore either I dare not let my children eat of that fish or else I give them great charge to take heed of bones, and when they eat of the pickerel also. But for this fish, my husband hath no great pleasure in them, and if he do bring any home, he will not eat of them if he have any other fish.

Pɪ. I do not much pass of [care for] any fish to eat, but that hunger forceth me sometimes and want of other things, and when I am weary (as

[61a] *better to fill my belly than mine eye*: proverbial. See Tilley G 146.

[62] *take mine ease in mine inn*: proverbial. See Tilley E 42.

[63] *chub . . . chevin*: interchangeable in Walton (pp. 99-104).

[D$_{iii}$^{v}] it were) of flesh.[64] And yet the chevin's head I do love very well, for next unto the carp's head it is the best and very sweet, if the mouth be clean washed.[65] But or ever I speak any further of him, I must tell you a story of the age of a luce or pike which Gesnerus[66] doth make report of with a ring about his neck, of this fashion hereafter drawn.[67]

In the year of our Lord 1497, a pike was taken in a lake about Haslepurn, the imperial city of Swethland,[68] and a ring of copper found in his gills, under his skin; and a little part thereof seen shining, whose figure and inscription about the compass of it was such in Greek as we here exhibit, which John Dalburg, Bishop of

[64] *flesh*: meat. Cf. the saying, "neither fish nor flesh."

[65] *if the mouth be clean washed*: i.e., the chevin's mouth. Cf. Walton, p. 104: ". . . the head of a large cheven, the throat being well washed, is the best part of him."

[66] *Gesnerus*: Konrad von Gesner (1516-65), Swiss naturalist, to whom Izaak Walton referred frequently. He was the author of the folio four-volume *Historia animalium*, printed at Zurich 1551-58 (German translation entitled *Thierbuch*, Zurich, 1563). *Encycl. Brit.* (ed. of 1953, X, 137) declares the *Historia* to have been "the starting point of modern Zoology." The present story is taken from his *Nomenclator aquatilium animantium*, Zurich, 1560, p. 316, according to D. E. Rhodes (*The Library*, 5th Series, X [1955], 123-24).

[67] *of this fashion hereafter drawn*: the drawing of the ring with its Greek inscription is printed on the first page of the facsimile text.

[68] *Haslepurn, the imperial city of Swethland*: the author, or his printer, has created confusion here, for no "Haslepurn" is known, and "Swethland" is a common sixteenth-century form of Sweden. What Gesner had written in the Latin account in his *Nomenclator aqua-tilium animantium*, according to D. E. Rhodes, *The Li-*

Worms,[69] did expound it thus: "I am the first fish of all, put into this lake by the hands of Frederick the Second,[70] ruler of the world, the fifth day of October, in the year of our Lord D_{iiii} —1230." Thereupon is gathered the sum of 267 years. And, verily, before it was of Frederick the Emperor so marked, a good while it had lived, and, if as yet it had not been taken, it would have lived a longer time.

And now to return to the chevin. When I dwelled in Savoy, the overmost[71] parts of Switzerland, in angling in a part of Losana Lake[72] and the ditch of Geneva,[73] but chiefly in the swift Rodanus,[74] I took sometime the chevin and very

---

brary, loc.cit., was "Haylpruñ imperialē Sueuiae urbem," that is, "Heilbron, the imperial city of Swabia," not Sweden. It is interesting that Walton also tells the story, though in an abbreviated form; he mentions no city, but says the fish was caught in "Swedeland." Was he led astray by our author?

[69] *John Dalburg, Bishop of Worms*: Johann von Dalberg (1445-1503) became bishop of Worms in 1482. He was a patron of humanistic studies and had devoted himself particularly to the study of Greek.

[70] *Frederick the Second*: Holy Roman Emperor (1194-1250).

[71] *overmost*: highest. The Alpes de Savoie include some of the highest peaks of the system, among them Mont Blanc and Monte Rosa.

[72] *Losana Lake*: Lake of Lausanne (Geneva).

[73] *ditch of Geneva*: in that portion of the Lake of Lausanne known as the Petit Lac, where it narrows to discharge the Rhone through the city of Geneva, there are some five deeper stretches in mid-channel. These fosses (pits, trenches) comprise the ditch of Geneva.

[74] *swift Rodanus*: through Geneva and beyond the environs of that city the Rhone flows with great speed. At Geneva its winter flow is some 7,000 cubic feet per second; in summer this is tripled.

fair, the people marveling at my pastime (for that recreation is not there used). They much more marveled that I or any of my countrymen would eat of them, for they do as much despise them as the Frieser in Friesland doth abhor to eat calves' flesh.[75]

VI. How kill you the chevin?

[D_{iiii}^v]   PI. He will bite very well at a minnow, the great red worm,[76] the white worm in the dead ash,[77] the grasshopper, the young unhaired mouse, the black snail, slit in the back that her grease may hang out, the hornet, the great bear

[75] *the Frieser . . . calves' flesh*: I have been unable to locate any contemporary reference to the Friesans' dislike of veal.

[76] *red worm*: An explanation is necessary on our author's use of the term "worm." His red worm, great red worm, red knotted worm, and great knotted red worm are all members of the *Lumbricidae*, angleworms or earthworms. We are all familiar with the red worm; we know of his diet of decaying leaves, his appearance on the surface of the ground after a night of drizzling rain, his generally reddish or pinkish coloration. The "knotted worm" is more difficult of diagnosis, but Mr. Pallister's interpretation seems correct. The word knotted implies that the worm is carrying an egg-capsule, whose smooth surface contrasting with the ring-like structure of the rest of the body, takes on the appearance of a cord with a knot in it. (See illustration of the earthworm on p. 1687 of *The Animal Kingdom*, Garden City, New York, vol. 3.) The words "small" and "great" applied to earthworms throughout the treatise refer simply to size or length, and indicate little difference in species, although a few specimens may be closely related species.

[77] *white worm in the dead ash*: the ash-borer (*Podosesia syringæ fraxini*, sp. *Lepidoptera*).

worm[78] in a swift stream or at a mill-tail[79] with heavy gears [strong tackle], the marrow in the ridge-bone of a loin of veal, yea, and rather than fail, at a piece of bacon, I mean the fat.

VI. I have heard say that he will not stick [hesitate] to bite at a frog.

PI. I know not that, but this I tell you, you must stand close, for he hath a quick eye and will fly like an arrow out of a bow to his den or hole, which he is never far from. Your line must be strong and your hook well hardened. Well, now, after grace we will sit by the fire.

VI. And have another fit.

PI. Sometime, with all the cunning that we have, we come home without, and take such as we find and not such as we bring, and then should we have best cheer made us.

VI. And why? For methinketh that then you do deserve worst.

PI. Nay, not so, for that were a double hurt, both to have evil luck abroad and worse at home; but as it is with hunters, so is it with us, for their rule is to fare best when they speed [succeed] not. The one reason why is this: that then they have taken most and longest pain; another is, that so are they well comforted after their unspeeding sport, and by that means encouraged the rather to go to it again to make some recompence. But what do I among hunters? If one of them heard

[78] *great bear worm*: great barley worm. Probably the army worm, the larva of a certain noctuid moth destructive to grain crops such as barley (bear).

[79] *at a mill-tail*: water which runs away from a mill-wheel and therefore very fast.

me, he would say *Ne ultra sutor crepidam.*[80] Say grace, maid.

[D_v^v]   ANNE. The God of peace which brought again from, &c.

PI. Now to the fire. Get him a chair, and now will we speak of angling for the carp.[81] He is a stout, heady fish, strong headed and tailed, and mightily boned and scaled, a fish not long known in England, but very dainty, and specially well baked, for then may ye eat him bones and all.

VI. Will he bite as well as other fish?

PI. Yea, but as his lair is: for if he be in a pond, he will bite all summer in a manner, saving in shelrode time, which some call spawning time, which time is forbidden to fish for any kind of fish.[82] He is not in many rivers. It hath not been heard of that the carp hath been found in any running water[83] or stream, but by heads of

[80] *Ne ultra sutor crepidam*: Let not the shoemaker go beyond his last. For the saying, cf. Valerius Maximus 8, 12, ext. 3.

[81] *carp*: *Cyprinus carpio*, introduced into England as early as the 14th century and commonly bred in ponds. (NED, sb.¹ 1.) Cf. Walton, p. 207: "The Carp is the queen of rivers: a stately, a good, and a very subtle fish, that was not at first bred, nor hath been long, in England, but is now naturalised." Dame Juliana Berners said of the carp that "there ben but fewe in Englonde." ("Piscator" ed., 1885, p. 25.)

[82] *forbidden to fish for any kind of fish*: though a great many ponds and streams were privately owned and guarded against poachers in the sixteenth century, there was no legal closed season. Our author, a good sportsman, does not fish in spawning season, the months of March, April, and May.

[83] *hath not . . . been found in any running water*: cf. Walton, p. 209: ". . . they breed more naturally in ponds than in running waters, if they breed there at all."

pools bursting out where carps have been, or land [D$_{vi}$]
floods that have overflowed such places, and so
they have been carried into rivers. As I know a
river myself where beyond sixteen years past there
was never heard of nor seen any carp by the
oldest man, and now there be so many that it is
no news for one man with his angle to kill in a
morning twenty or forty. Yea, there is such store
that, for my part, I would there were fewer; they
bear such a sway in the river that all other fish
are almost gone. They may be compared to some
stout, needy upstarts, for though they cannot
raven and destroy their fellows (unless it be a
poor minnow) yet, with countenance[84] and shouldering, other fish will not gladly be where they
abound. Their first coming into this river was
surely by some great flood which came out of
Buckinghamshire and Bedfordshire,[85] which [D$_{vi}$^{v}]
shires are well furnished with carp. But now have
they settled themselves with us and do breed, so
that at some rising of waters beneath us they do
take them in by [at] ditches by coulefuls [tub
fulls], of a span[86] long, and upward. Our fens be
now full. You shall have an hundred of goodly
store fish[87] of one foot apiece in length for five
shillings.

VI. Well, now, I pray you, to the taking of
him.

---

[84] *countenance*: display of ill will.

[85] *Buckinghamshire and Bedfordshire*: mention of these
shires identifies the river as the Ouse, which rises in
Oxfordshire near Brackley and flows through Buckinghamshire and Bedfordshire before entering the county of
Huntingdon.

[86] *span*: 9 inches.

[87] *store fish*: fish to keep for a supply.

[51]

' Pi. In the river he will bite chiefly in August and all September. His bite is in the morning and late at the night. I know but two baits for him; the one is the great red worm, the other is bread.[88] Some say new-baked rye bread, and some say white bread, but this I do know by experience, that look what bread you use him to in feeding of him, that shall ye take him withal.

[Dvii] Vi. Why, must you feed him?

Pi. Yea, that you must, either in pool or running river, though in the fens there is such store that, where any little void plot is for leaves,[89] you cannot put in your bait amiss, as I have heard.

Vi. But, I pray you, how shall I feed them?

Pi. You must take with you a good shiver [fragment] of bread in a fair linen bag or cloth, and when you come to your place, take a piece and chew it in your mouth until it be moist, and then ball it and cast it in where your float shall be, and so two or three mouthsful, if you will, whiles you are a making of your tools ready. Then bait your hook with the same chewed bread, this added to, that that which you bait withal be labored in your palm of your left hand with the thumb of your right hand, but [Dvii v] look that it be neither too tough nor too brittle, for they be both hurtful.

Vi. How so?

Pi. If the bait be tough and hardish like stiff dough, then it is too hard for the hook to go easily through, specially when the bite is not

---

[88] *two baits . . . worm . . . bread*: cf. Walton, p. 215: "the carp bites either at worms or at paste."

[89] *void plot is for leaves*: any small stretch of water free of arrowhead or pond lilies.

fast, and so the fish letteth it go as it came, or grateth a little in her mouth, and so hurteth the pastime, the toughness of the bread pulling it off, that the hook cannot fully strike at the first, unless you strike hard, and that again is dangerous for breaking of your line, tearing of her lip, knapping [snapping] asunder of the small end of your angle, and, last of all, the sudden moving of the water, with the sight of your gears, which will make the fish shy and fearful.

VI. What other bait have you for him?

PI. The great worm is also a good bait, as I [D$_{viii}$] said, lying a foot on the ground, as the bread must, and a bob of gentles he will bite at sometimes.

VI. When biteth he best?

PI. I told you, in August and September. Strike not until you see him go away with the bait by pulling down of your float; and if your bready bait be brittle, as mingled with barley or not well kneaded in your hand, then the small fish will nibble it off. Thus have I spoken of the killing of the carp in the river. And in the pond or moat the baits afore be good, so that you meat[90] a plat or two or more, as you shall think good, evening and morning, with bread, grains, and blood mingled together, or ground malt. And cut with a long pole and a hook the weeds away a good compass for fear of his running into them; and be sure that your line be strong, as [D$_{viii}$^{v}] of green silk or hair, of sixteen or twenty hairs in the line. In the pond he will bite at all times in the summer, saving in shelrode time, as I said.

[90] *meat*: supply with food.

VI. But, sir, I pray you, what bait have you for killing of the house carp, now you have spoken of the river carp and the pond carp?

PI. The best bait that ever I did know for the killing of that carp is a quantity of sufferance, with a good deal of patience,[91] and as much silence as may be possible, all these well mingled together; and so go your way, if you see that there be no remedy.

VI. Why, some hold that those carps are best killed with an angle made of an hazel wand, without a line.[92]

PI. Indeed, some do use it, but whether they kill the carps or catch more carps that way or no, that I have no experience of and, therefore, can say little.

VI. Well, I know some that, if they should not use that kind of angling, they should not be without store of carps, both at bed and at board.[93]

PI. Yea, but then they be cloyed with pouts, which is an ill-favored fish. And if there be no remedy, rather give me the carp than the pout,

91 *sufferance, with a good deal of patience*: cf. Walton, p. 214: "if you will fish for a carp, you must put on a very large measure of patience," and, p. 215, "being possessed with that hope and patience, which I wish to all fishers, especially to the carp-angler."

92 *hazel wand, without a line*: since carp often lie near the surface, they can be killed from a boat or the bank by striking them with a hazel rod.

93 *carps, both at bed and at board*: Viator puns on carp, (1) fish and (2) complaining speech. The phrase *at bed and at board* shows that he is referring to his wife. Piscator caps his pun with the word *pout*, (1) a fish, eel-pout, *lota vulgaris*, and (2) a protrusion of the lips expressive of annoyance.

although I like neither, for the head of the one
is better than the liver of the other. But now to
leave this kind of carping, let us now pass on to
speak further of angling.

Vᵢ. Content. How kill you the bream?

Pᵢ. At the ground with a red worm, the gentle,
brown bread, and the oak worm.⁹⁴ He is heady
and heavy, but soon checked; he biteth but
seldom, and that daintily, loath to be hurt, and
flieth if you miss him with touching, as I will tell
you a strange tale of a bream that was taken in
our river, called the Ouse, which bream I bought. [Eᵛ]

Vᵢ. Was she taken in a net or with an angle?

Pᵢ. With a net, in drawing the water at Huntingdon bridge,⁹⁵ and when she should be put into
a trunk⁹⁶ (as I willed [her] for a time to be kept
alive) the hole was with the least,⁹⁷ for she was
a very great fish of a bream, both in breadth and
thickness, as ever I saw; and so with struggling she
slipped into the water and away she went, which
grieved me somewhat.

⁹⁴ *red worm etc.*: Walton's recommendations (pp. 220-
21) are practically identical, though he does not mention
the oak worm, which is the grub of the acorn weevil,
Curculio, sp. *Coleoptera.*

⁹⁵ *Huntingdon bridge*: the present bridge spanning the
Ouse was erected in 1332. It "is of six arches and faced with
ashlar. The parapets are carried round the outer edge of
the piers, forming refuges for foot passengers, those at the
northern end being triangular and those at the southern
end semi-hexagonal." (*Victoria History of the County of
Huntingdon,* London, 1932, II, 125.)

⁹⁶ *trunk*: a perforated floating box in which live fish
are kept. (NED, *trunk,* sb. 2. 8.)

⁹⁷ *the hole was with the least*: the hole in the trunk
was cut for the insertion of a bream of the smallest size.

VI. I blame you not.

PI. Yet God sent her me again, for within three or four days afterward the water beneath us also was drawn at a town called Saint Tyves,[98] three mile from us by land but four good mile by water, and there was that selfsame bream taken again, and so I was fain to buy her the second time.

VI. But, I pray you, how did you know that it was she and none other?

PI. By two marks: one was that on the side of her head, under the gill, she had a great red wen as broad as a tester,[99] and also I had cut off a piece of her tail.

VI. Now, surely, it was strange.

PI. It was so, for I have seen the contrary in other fish, as once I did see a good perch struck and long tugged withal, and when she was ready to be landed, the over end of the hook had so fretted the hair[100] that it brake, and away she went; and the party, fastening on another hook, laid in again, and surely within an hour after the same perch did bite again. He struck her and had her with the hook in her lip that she had gone away withal afore. With which two examples I have learned that some fish hath better memories than other some have, or one more fearful than another.

VI. I have heard of another bait or twain that is good for the bream.

[E₁₁] water

[E₁₁ᵛ] gone

---

[98] *Saint Tyves*: local pronunciation of St. Ives, five miles east of the town of Huntingdon.

[99] *tester*: a colloquial or slang term for sixpence.

[100] *hair*: of the line.

Modernized Text

Pɪ. Ye say true, the flag worm and the bob under the cow turd.[101]

Vɪ. The flag worm, how come you by her?

Pɪ. You must pull up flags by the roots out of the water, and in the roots you shall find white worms as big as gentles, and they be very good. Yea, I may say to you for the carp also; but that everybody may not know it, for that is a secret. And in the roots of the rush you shall find good baits also. But now to the dace.

Vɪ. Well said. I pray you, how do you angle for him?

Pɪ. Two ways, above and beneath: for from June until September he will bite above at the fly,[102] without lead or float, or with a small quill without lead, and within two foot of the fly. You must have a long line; you must stand close and throw with the wind and with the stream, your eye being very good, and a ready hand, with a long hazel wand or other trim straight wand, for a reed is not good. E_{iii}

Vɪ. How many hairs at that hook must I have?

Pɪ. You may have two or three hairs, because that your stroke, the swift bite of the fish, and

101 *flag worm and the bob under the cow turd*: These are probably young larvae of the iris borer, or water-flag borer, *Macronoctua*, sp. *Lepidoptera*. The name is also used in some places for the dock-worm, which Mr. Weiss suggests may have the meaning "wharf-borer," i.e., borer found in iris near the wharf. The *bob under the cow turd* is a dipterous maggot. There are many flies belonging to the order *Diptera* which deposit eggs in cow-manure.

102 *bite above at the fly*: our author's only account of wet-fly fishing. Cf. Walton, pp. 276-77, "They will bite almost at any fly, but especially at ant-flies."

against the stream, as you must strike, the line
had need be of some strength. And the fish must
also be considered: for if you come among great
daces (as I have seen some as big as a fresh
herring full),[103] then shall you find three hairs
with the least, and they had need to be good, well
twisted,[104] and without frets.[105]

Vɪ. They may not be she hairs[106] then?

[E[iii]ᵛ]   Pɪ. No, indeed, for they be not good; they be
so often moistened. Neither is the gelding hair
so good, but of these matters hereafter. After
September until the midst of February at the very
ground he will bite, either at the red worm,
gentle, oak worm, or malt corn, yea, at the very
ground; trailing on it in a gravely place is best,
and then with one hair.

Vɪ. Why, all those months be in a manner
winter months, and I had thought that then your
angles had shrouded.[107]

Pɪ. No, no, then is the chiefest angling. I have
on Twelfth Even[108] and on Candlemas Even[109]
taken such messes of fish with mine angle as hath
passed [defied description]. Yea, in frost and
snow, when the icicles hath hanged at mine angle

103 *herring full*: a herring charged with roe. (NED,
full, adj. A, 1. e.)

104 *twisted*: plaited, woven together.

105 *frets*: a decayed spot in a hair. (NED, *fret*, sb.² 1.)

106 *she hairs*: I can find no evidence to support the
belief that the hair of mares and geldings is less effective
than stallion hair and am inclined to put it down as an
angling superstition.

107 *shrouded*: sought shelter.

108 *Twelfth Even*: January 5th.

109 *Candlemas Even*: February 1st.

top, I have had best sport. When he bites, if you
light of the skull,[110] he bites sure and is a heady[111]
fish to land; and if he wrestle with you, have him   E_iiii
out of your plat[112] as much as you may to tire him,
for hurting of your game. Well, now to the roach.

Vi. How kill you her?

Pi. In summer with the red worm, until it be
about Michaelmas,[113] and then the malt corn,
and after, the gentle. That fish is the common fish
and easily killed: she is very simple, and the plat
being well meated[114] with balls, you shall fill
your pail at a plat, if the scar[115] come not.

Vi. What is that?

Pi. The pike or pickerel.

Vi. How shall I know when he is come?

Pi. By casting in of your meat, which may be
unballed if the water be still, for immediately
after, you shall see the small fish fly suddenly
every way, and sometimes above the water, and
he after.

Vi. Then the sport is marred?

Pi. That is true, but for every sore there is a [E_iiii^v]
salve.[116] You must have a pike hook ready, and
put on a small roach with a good strong line and
a float, having a spare rod by you, and cast it in;

110 *light of the skull*: drop the bait on the crown or top
of the head.

111 *heady*: violent.

112 *plat*: locality; here "the water over which you fish."

113 *Michaelmas*: September 29th.

114 *the plat being well meated*: the ground bait having
been generously scattered.

115 *scar*: pike, as the following dialogue shows. The word
must have been of only local currency.

116 *for every sore . . . a salve*: Tilley S 84.

let it lie by you until he bite, and so shall you have him. It may be that your sport is hurt also with a great perch or two, and then a gudgeon or a minnow is very good, with a strong single hook cast in with a spare rod lying by you, as before. But in winter, as about Christmas, Candlemas, and Lent, if the water be not frozen over, until the fish go to rode [spawn], the red worm is very good, but chiefly the white worm that breedeth between the bark and the wood of an oak, with a little red, hard head.[117] In shides [splintered pieces] of oak that stand upright or lie dry they commonly be, which have been two years felled. And sometimes you shall have them in the wood, and those be commonly great and fair; then must you rend them out.

E_v VI. And have you no other bait for the roach?

PI. Yes, blood is very good.

VI. What, any manner of blood?

PI. No, not so.

VI. What blood then?

PI. Sheep's blood.[118]

VI. But how do you make it abide on the hook?

PI. You must have a pretty flat box, such a one as round trenchers be put in—I mean the cover, for that is deep enough—or of an marmalade

117 *white worm . . . hard head*: the cambium borer (*Conotrachelus*, sp. *Coleoptera*). Walton, p. 275, disagrees on the bait for winter roaching: "you shall fish for this in winter with paste or gentles."

118 *Sheep's blood*: cf. Walton, p. 279, "and so also is the thick blood of sheep, being half-dried on a trencher." Walton goes on to describe, more concisely than our author, the process of making bait out of dried sheep's blood.

box. And when the sheep is killed, let the box be filled with the blood that runneth out of the sheep's throat. And then when it is cold, turn it out upon a trencher, that the water may drain from it two or three hours; then put it into your box again, and so take it with you to angle withal.

Vi. What, must I put it on whole?

Pi. Yea, if you fish for a codshead,[119] which you need not.

Vi. Lo, now you be angry! [E$_v$^{v}]

Pi. Why, hath a man heard such a reason? You will never, I fear me, be [a] good angler. Have you no more wit than so, or spake you in jest?

Vi. In jest I spake, indeed.

Ci. Yea, but I can tell you my husband hath cast off many, and that some of his chiefest acquaintances, for their jesting when he talketh of his cunning in angling. But I pray you, good sirs, when will ye to bed? The night is far spent.

Vi. Well then, God be with you until another time. I will remember where we left, at our next meeting.

Vi. Are you within?

Pi. What, are you come so soon? Come near, I pray you.

Vi. God give you good morrow. Yea, at your business so soon?

Pi. I am making of a new line. Sit you down. [E$_{vi}$] Can you tell where we left?

119 *codshead*: blockhead, stupid fellow. Piscator loses his temper at the last question.

VI. Or else it were strange, for I have been an angling all night in my dreams.

PI. Nay, then you will prove an angler indeed!

VI. Your last talk was of carrying of blood in a box with me when I go a-fishing. How shall I use it when I come to my fishing plat?

PI. You must have a trencher with you: and lay your blood upon it, and then cut it over and over again, like jelly, with the point of your knife, so that your pieces be like unto square dice. And then put a piece on your hook—it will be tough enough—and throw in now and then some by[120] to eat freely. And if your blood do begin to look black, you must have a little salt about you, and sprinkle your blood with it, and it will make it [E_{vi}^v] not only red but also tough. But I tell you, you must be very ready in your stroke, and nimble, with a diligent, quick eye, for this bait is lost at every bite, catch or not catch.

VI. But is here all your baits for the roach?

PI. All? No, not by a number, which hereafter, both as I see you delight in the pastime and [as] memory shall move me, you shall know of them. Notwithstanding, one bait that is a simple I will tell you that passeth [exceeds belief], if you can order it.

VI. I pray you, let us have it, and so a word or two of the ordering of your baits afore spoken of and promised; and then, an end for this time.

PI. The bait that I now will tell you of is so fine that a prince may deal with it. You must take

---

120 *throw in now and then some by*: scatter some pieces around, as ground bait.

a handful of well-made malt[121] and rub it between your hands in a fair dish of water to make them as clean as you may. Then, in a small vessel of water, seethe them simpering-wise [let them simmer] until they be somewhat soft, which you shall discern by feeling of one of them between your finger and your thumb; then take them off and drain the water from them. Then must you have a fine knife and sharp, turning up the sprout end of the corn upward, and with the point of your knife take off the back part or husk first, leaving another husk notwithstanding, or else all $[\text{E}_{\text{vii}}]$

[121] *handful of well-made malt*: I quote at full length Walton's description of the preparation of the malt bait for roach (p. 278). The phrasing of the two descriptions is so closely similar that borrowing by Walton seems the most reasonable way of accounting for it.
". . . get a handful of well-made malt, and put it into a dish of water, and then wash and rub it betwixt your hands till you make it clean, and as free from husks as you can; then put that water from it, and put a small quantity of fresh water to it, and set it in something that is fit for that purpose over the fire, where it is not to boil apace, but leisurely and very softly, until it become somewhat soft, which you may try by feeling it betwixt your finger and thumb; and when it is soft, then put your water from it: then take a sharp knife, and turning the sprout-end upward, with the point of your knife take the back part of the husk off from it, and yet leaving a kind of inward husk on the corn, or else it is marred; and then cut off that sprouted end, I mean a little of it, that the white may appear, and so pull off the husk on the cloven side, as I directed you; and then cutting off a very little of the other end, that so your hook may enter; and, if your hook be small and good, you will find this to be a very choice bait, either for winter or summer, you sometimes casting a little of it into the place where your float swims."

is marred. Then cut off that sprouted end a little, that the white may appear, and so pull off the husk on the cloven side, as afore. And then cut off a little of the nether end, so putting it on your hook, which must be very fine, made of card wire,[122] and cover the point of your hook in the cleft of your malt corn, beard and all. Then thrust out between your finger and thumb's end the white of the corn a little, that the fish may see it.

Vi. Is this so notable a bait?

[E~vii~ᵛ] Pi. This bait cometh in at September and lasteth four months well. With this bait I have killed roachs as big as my foot and of fifteen, sixteen, and seventeen inches long, with one hair.

Vi. It will be a good while or ever I shall come to that cunning. But now I do remember me, you have not yet spoken of the killing of the tench, the barbel, and the trout.

Pi. It is true. Let these suffice you, friend, for I will speak of those and other in my next addition, though I dare not well deal in the angling of the trout, for displeasing of one of our wardens,[123] which either is counted the best trouter in England, or so thinketh, who would not (as I suppose) have the taking of that fish common. But yet thus much I may say, that he worketh with a fly in a box.

122 *card wire*: presumably the wire used in making bristles for wool carding.

123 *one of our wardens*: not what is called in the United States a fish-warden, but probably a warden (i.e., a member of the governing body) of Piscator's guild, or a church warden, or a market warden, or a way warden. The way wardens were appointed to take charge of the repair of a bridge or highway, and to make regulations for its use.

Vi. Now, I pray you, to the ordering of your baits.

Pi. Your red worms must be scoured in moss, [E$_{viii}$] finkel [fennel], or cammamell [camomile] in a little comfit box,[124] a day or a night before you occupy [use] them. The case worm you may gather in ditches with a long stick cloven at the end to hold them until you bring them up. Then put them in a little linen or woolen bag. You may gather enough to serve you two or three days; putting them in a close vessel with fair [fresh] water and a little sand in the bottom, your worm will keep a fortnight very well.

Vi. But how make you gentles, to keep them?

Pi. Of a piece of a beast's liver,[125] hanged in some corner over a pot or little barrel, with a cross stick and the vessel half full of red clay; and as they wax big, they will fall into that troubled clay and so scour them that they will

124 *comfit box*: candy or sweetmeat box.

125 *beast's liver*: Walton's instructions for keeping gentles immediately precedes his discussion of malt bait. See note 121. Again Walton is so close to our author as to suggest that he is borrowing. Walton says (p. 278), "take a piece of beast's liver, and with a cross stick hang it in some corner over a pot or barrel, half full of dry clay; and as the gentles grow big, they will fall into the barrel, and scour themselves, and be always ready for use whensoever you incline to fish; and these gentles may be thus created till after Michaelmas. But if you desire to keep gentles to fish with all the year, then get a dead cat or a kite, and let it be fly-blown; and when the gentles begin to be alive and to stir, then bury it and them in soft, moist earth, but as free from frost as you can, and these you may dig up at any time when you intend to use them; these will last till March, and about that time turn to be flies."

be ready at all times. These you may make until All-Hallowstide[126] from time to time, and then a cat, a buzzard, or a dead swan, full-blown[127] and [E_{viii}^v] buried in the earth. You shall there have all winter such gentles as you shall kill when others go without, and they will last until March and then fly.[128] It is time I were gone.

VI. Well, if you hie you not apace, I will be at the river before you.

F I N I S

Imprinted at London in
Fleet Street at the sign of the
Falcon by Henry Middleton[129]
and are to be sold at his
shop in St. Dun-
stan's church-
yard.

Anno 1577

126 *All-Hallowstide*: November 1st.
127 *full-blown*: in complete decay.
128 *and then fly*: the grubs, having developed into maturity, will fly off.
129 *Henry Middleton*: He was a fairly well-known Elizabethan printer. Since his father, William Middleton, was a member of the company, Henry was admitted to the Stationers' Company by patrimony in 1567. After a short partnership with Thomas East, young Middleton set up for himself in 1572, and was admitted to the livery of the company in 1577. In 1587 he was elected one of the two wardens, or responsible directors of the company, and in September of that year he died.

The Context of
The Arte of Angling

The genealogy of English fishing books is long and complicated,[1] but for most readers—as for most fishermen—there is one ancestor which attracts all pious veneration. In 1653 Izaak Walton published the book which he called *The Compleat Angler, or the Contemplative Man's Recreation. Being a Discourse of Fish and Fishing, Not unworthy the perusal of most Anglers.* He corrected, revised, and expanded it in editions of 1655, 1661, 1668, and 1676, the last of which contains his final revisions and is the basis of nearly three hundred later editions.[2] (These later editions often include his friend Charles Cotton's book on trout fishing, which was first issued with Walton's 1676 edition.)

Six English predecessors of Walton's book have long been known, most of them known well enough to appear in modern reprints and facsimiles. The six are:

1) [Dame Juliana Barnes?] *the treatyse of fysshynge wyth an Angle.* [Added to the second edition of *The Book of St. Albans,* 1496.]

[1] See D. Mulder Bosgoed, *Bibliotheca ichthyologica et piscatoria,* 1874, and Thomas Westwood and T. Satchell, *A New Bibliotheca Piscatoria, or, General Catalogue of Angling and Fishing Literature.* 1883.

[2] See Arnold Wood, *A Bibliography of "The Complete Angler."* New York, 1900; and Peter Oliver, *A New Chronicle of the Compleat Angler.* New York, 1936.

2) L[eonard] M[ascall] *A Booke of fishing with Hooke & Line, and of all other instruments thereunto belonging . . . Made by L. M.* 1590.

3) John Taverner. *Certaine Experiments Concerning Fish and Frvite: Practised by Iohn Taverner Gentleman, and by him published for the benefit of others.* 1600. [Not really an angling book, but a treatise on the making, stocking, and management of fish ponds.]

4) J[ohn] D[ennys] *The Secrets of Angling: Teaching, The choisest Tooles Baytes and seasons, for the taking of any Fish, in Pond or Riuer: practised and familiarly opened in three Bookes. By I. D. Esquire* . . . 1613.

5) G[ervase] M[arkham] *The Pleasures of Princes, Or Good mens Recreations: Containing a Discourse of the generall Art of Fishing with the Angle, or otherwise: and of all the hidden secrets belonging thereunto* . . . 1614.

6) Thomas Barker. *The Art of Angling. Wherein are discovered many rare secrets, very necessary to be known by all that delight in that Recreation. Written by Thomas Barker, an ancient Practitioner in the said Art.* 1651.

As one would expect in the literature of a cherished pastime, these books are comprised largely of traditional lore with the addition of individual observations and practises. Most of them show knowledge and use of (though seldom acknowledgment to) *the treatyse of fysshynge wyth an Angle*. Mascall's lucidly organized and presented manual is at times a paraphrase of it, while Markham's book is largely a compilation from *the treatyse*, Mascall, and Dennys. The prolific Markham's periodic reissues of revised, reorganized, or merely re-named books of his own and other men's composition are notorious. Other popular writers of the time were only a little less irrepressible.

When *The Compleat Angler* appeared in 1653, it too showed use of preceding angling books. Walton cited Dennys (B_6^v and D_2-D_3), Markham (B_6^v), Barker (I_2^v), and Mascall (M_1), and he quoted Dennys (D_2-D_3) and Barker (H_6^v-H_7). In other parts of his book he pretty surely made less obvious use of his predecessors.

These borrowings are, however, slight and insignificant, both in the light of current practices and in regard to the striking differences between his book and the earlier ones. Though many of the same subjects are treated in all of them, the fundamental structure and method of *The Compleat Angler* are quite different from those used in the other six. *The treatyse of fysshynge wyth an Angle*, for example, is a simple manual, with an introduction on the antiquity of fishing and a conclusion made up of a set of six admonitions for the good angler. Mascall's book is the manual *par excellence*, with a lucid organization and copious rubrics and illustrations. Taverner is not an angler at all, but an agriculturalist and a conservationist who presents advice for the development of estates. Dennys is most like Walton, for he is imbued with the beauty of nature and the joys of fishing, but he writes a didactic poem, and he has no characters and no dialogue. Markham is, as in many of his other books, a compiler, and he adds little to his predecessors, often merely paraphrasing Mascall. Barker writes very personally out of his own experience, particularly in the preparing and cooking of fish. He is wholly practical and matter-of-fact; he says firmly, "You must take a line," "You must take half Claret-Wine."

And then we come to Izaak Walton's book, which reads quite differently from any of these earlier ones. The first edition of 1653 (which was altered and much expanded in later and more familiar editions) is a rather small book of thirteen short chapters containing a narrative which envelopes teaching in the delights of story and description. In structure it is a dialogue between Piscator and his friend Viator (renamed Venator in later editions), whom he meets by chance and keeps with him for several days of fishing, interspersed with the eating of fish and fish talk at the inns to which they bring their catch. Most of the dialogue consists of Piscator's explanations of the antiquity and the art of fishing and of the habits of fish—explanations which he makes in response to the questions of Viator, who becomes his pupil. The basic pattern of the little book is varied by the occasional introduction of other characters, such as the Hunters, the Hostess, the Milkwoman and her daughter Maudlin, and two other fishermen called Peter and Coridon, and it is made delightful by the insertion of anecdotes and a score of songs and poems. In later editions these descants and variations are further elaborated, and they have come to constitute for many readers the essential charm of the book.

But it is Walton's original version of 1653 and its basic structure which I should like to discuss a little further—this dialogue between Viator and Piscator, who meet by chance and discuss fishing, with Piscator in the role of teacher and Viator in that of pupil. It is this basic structure which differentiates *The Compleat Angler* most sharply from those earlier English fishing books that had already set out most of Walton's facts about angling. They had all been without dialogue, without impersonation, and, except for three scattered passages in Barker, without narrative. Walton abandoned the precedent of the earlier English fishing books when he used dialogue and impersonation as his fundamental structural device and when he added the conversion of an infidel to the faith of the fisherman for what might be called plot interest. These elements, which give to *The Compleat Angler* much of its distinction, appeared to be Walton's own contribution to fishing literature.

Then two or three years ago another early English angling book was discovered.[3] The appearance of a totally unknown and unsuspected printed book of the sixteenth century—one of

[3] It was first noted in print when the unique copy, then on deposit in the British Museum, was described in a short note by D. E. Rhodes. *Library*. Fifth Series. X (1955), 123-25.

which there is no record in any list of lost books, no entry in the Stationers' Register, to which there is not even any allusion—the recovery of such a publication on any subject is surprising. That it should belong to a class of books which has been collected avidly, as angling books have been collected for a century and more, might almost be ranked with fishermen's tales of the one that got away.

But fisherman's tale or not, there is such a forerunner for *The Compleat Angler.* The unique copy was bought by Mr. Otto v. Kienbusch and generously presented to the Princeton University Library.[4] The book, whose running title is *The Arte of Angling*, must have consisted originally of forty leaves of black-letter text (A-E$_8$) and an unknown number of leaves of front matter. There remain thirty-seven leaves of text (B$_8$, C$_3$, and C$_4$ are missing) and one leaf which comes before the text and contains a sketch of the inscribed copper ring found on the 267-year-old pike that is described on D$_{iii}$^{v} and D$_{iiii}$ of the text. This page with the sketch was once preceded in this binding by at least three other leaves, the stubs of which are still visible. Perhaps one of these stubs may be the remainder of the title-page of the complete original, with the full title and the name of the author; the other two stubs may possibly be the remains of leaves containing an address to the reader, or a dedication, or a commendatory statement. If these stubs are the fragments of

[4] A limited facsimile edition was published for the Friends of the Princeton Library in December 1956.

preliminary leaves for *The Arte of Angling*, it is odd that the only remaining complete leaf is signed D_{iiii}, for the signatures on preliminary leaves did not ordinarily duplicate signatures to be used on following pages. This peculiarity led Mr. Rhodes to suggest in his note on the book in the *Library* that the leaves for the three stubs—perhaps D_i, D_{ii}, and D_{iii}—with D_{iiii} could have belonged to another book. If so, that book must have been related to *The Arte of Angling*, for the sketch on this preliminary D_{iiii} illustrates the story recounted in the text proper on D_{iii}^v-D_{iiii}.

Another interpretation of the evidence is that of Dr. Henry L. Savage, who has suggested that the sketch of the inscribed copper ring was intended to be an illustration for *The Arte of Angling*, and that the signature D_{iiii} indicates the appropriate location for the illustration in the text. His evidence is that in telling the story of the aged pike the author says on D_{iii}^v that the inscription on the copper ring "was such in greeke as we here exhibit." The phrase "here exhibite" leads me to prefer Dr. Savage's interpretation of the signature.

Since we lack a title-page for the book, we have no author's name and no certain title, though it could have been either the drop-head title, "A dialogue betweene Viator and Piscator," or the running-title, "The Arte of Angling." The latter —used both by Markham thirty-seven years later as the running-title for the angling section of *The Pleasures of Princes*, 1614, and by Thomas Barker as the title for his own fishing book seventy-four years later in 1651—seems to me somewhat more likely to have been the proper title of the book of 1577, though it is, of course, entirely possible that the lost title-page used still a third designation. Fortunately there is no doubt about the printer and the date of publication, both of which are given in the colophon:

> Imprinted at London in Fleetestreate at the signe of the Faulcon by Henrie Middleton and are to be sold at his shoppe in S. Dunstones churchyarde. *Anno 1577.*

This little book, the unique survivor of Henry Middleton's stock, shows rather hard use. Besides various miscellaneous scribbles, such as the repeated list of the months of the year on the verso of the D_{iiii} illustration, the volume bears the names of three of its owners:

> D_{iiii} [within the illustration] Thomas Dale His ffishing Booke   Anno Dom 88 [1688? 1788?]
> Eli Bakers Fishing Book Stoke on trent Staffordshire Septr 1841
> D_{ii}^{v} Robert Stapleton his booke Scibende [?] 6 day of Marche
> E_{iii}^{v} Robert Stapleton His Booke Anno Dommini 1646

The Robert Stapleton who owned the book in 1646 could have been the second son of the Presbyterian leader, Sir Philip, or he could have been the Robert Stapleton who is said to have been Oliver Cromwell's chaplain, or he could have been the translator and dramatist of that name. But neither of his names is very uncommon, especially in Yorkshire,[5] and further evidence would be required to associate the copy with any of the known Stapletons. Some owner of the book—the hand is not that of Dale, Baker, or Stapleton and appears to be earlier than any of them—has made a rough marginal index to the discussions of the various types of fish and their bait. In the margin of $C_v{}^v$ has been written "the ruf   the rufe hathe but one bate"; of C_{vii} "6 bates for the Parch   the Perch"; of $C_{viii}{}^v$ "fiue bates for the pickrell"; of $D_{iiii}{}^v$ "ten bates for the chevin"; of $D_v{}^v$ "the carpe"; of $D_{vi}{}^v$ "too bates for the carpe"; of E_i "foure bates for the brime"; of $E_{ii}{}^v$ "5 bates for the daces"; of E_{iiii} "4 bates for the roch"; and of $E_{vii}{}^v$ "the ordering of bates."

Whatever the fate of the other copies of Thomas Middleton's 1577 edition of this book, there can be no doubt that Izaak Walton had seen one of them. The evidence is fairly conclusive. In the first edition of his *Compleat Angler* Walton gives directions for keeping gentles:

> Take a piece of beasts liver and with a cross stick, hang it in some corner over a pot or barrell half full of dry clay, and as the Gentles grow big, they wil fall into the barrel, and scowre themselves, and be always ready for use whensoever you incline to fish; and these Gentles may be thus made til after *Michaelmas*: But if you desire to keep Gentles to fish with all the yeer, then get a

[5] See H. E. Chetwynd-Stapylton, *The Stapeltons of Yorkshire*. London, 1897, passim.

dead *Cat* or a *Kite*, and let it be fly-blowne, and when the Gentles begin to be alive and to stir, then bury it and them in moist earth, but as free from frost as you can, and these you may dig up at any time when you intend to use them; these wil last till *March*, and about that time turn to be flies. (1653 edition, $P_8{}^v$.)

Seventy-six years before, the unknown author of *The Arte of Angling* had published his directions for keeping gentles:

Of a peece of a beastes liuer, hanged in some corner ouer a pot, or little barrell, with a crosse sticke and the vessell halfe full of red Clay, and as they waxe big, they will fall into that troubled clay, and so scoure thē, that they will be readie at all times, these you may make vntill Alhallontide, frō time to time, & then a Cat, a Bussard, or a dead swan, ful blowen, and buried in the earthe, you shall there haue all Winter suche ientils, as you shall kill when others goe without, and they will laste vntill Marche, and then flie. (E_{viii}-$E_{viii}{}^v$.)

Similarly Walton gives directions for the preparation of malt bait for taking roach:

Get a handful of well made Mault, and put it into a dish of water, and then wash and rub it betwixt your hands til you make it cleane, and as free from husks as you can; then put that water from it, and put a smal quantitie of fresh water to it, and set it in

something that is fit for that purpose, over
the fire, where it is not to boil apace, but
leisurely, and very softly, until it become
somewhat soft, which you may try by feeling
it betwixt your finger and thumb; and when
it is soft, then put your water from it, then
take a sharp knife, and turning the sprout
end of the corn upward, with the point of
your knife take the back part of the husk off
from it, and yet leaving a kind of husk on
the corn, or else it is marr'd; and then cut off
that sprouted end (I mean a little of it) that
the white may appear, and so pull off the
husk on the cloven side (as I directed you)
and then cutting off a very little of the other
end, that so your hook may enter, and if
your hook be small and good, you will find
this to be a very choice bait either for Winter or Summer, you sometimes casting a little
of it into the place where your flote swims.
(1653 edition, $P_8{}^v$-$Q_1{}^v$.)

The instructions for the making of malt bait
in order to take roach in the little book of 1577
read:

You must take a hādful of well made malt,
& rub it betweene your hands in a fair dish
of water to make thē as clean as you may,
thē in a small vessel of water, seeth thē
simpering wise, vntil they be somewhat softe,
whiche you shall discerne by feeling of one
of them between your finger and your
thumbe, then take them off and dreane the
water from them, thē must you haue a fine

knife, and sharp, turning vp ye sprout ende of the corne vpward, and with the point of your knife, take of the backe part or houske first, leauing another houske notwithstanding, or else all is marred, then cut off that sprouted end a little, that the white may appeare, and so pull off the houske, on the clouen side, as afore, and then cutte off a little of the nether end, so putting it on your hook, which must be very fine, made of card wyre, and couer the point of your hooke in the cleft of your malt corne, beard & all, then thrust out betwene your finger and thumbs end, the white of y^e corn a little, that the fish may see it. (E$_{vi}$^{v}-E$_{vii}$.)

It might be thought that further evidence of Walton's indebtedness is to be seen in the fact that he repeats, with fewer details, the story of the fabulously aged pike (1653 edition, K$_8$) which is told and illustrated in *The Arte of Angling* (D$_{iii}$^{v}-D$_{iiii}$). I doubt, however, if this is evidence of further borrowings in *The Compleat Angler*, for Walton cites Gesner—whom he mentions frequently throughout his book—as his source. Mr. Rhodes has noted that *The Arte of Angling*, which also cites Gesner as the source, has taken the story with the Greek inscriptions on the copper rings from Gesner's *Nomenclator aquatilium animantium*, Tiguri, 1560. It is odd that *The Arte of Angling* says that the pike was taken in "Swethland," and that Walton says it was taken in "Swedeland." Both are wrong; Gesner had said "Sueuiae" or Swabia, which fits the geographical backgrounds of the Emperor Frederick the Second and of John Dalburg, Bishop of Worms, as Sweden does not. It is possible that Walton was led into error here by his use of *The Arte of Angling,* but his extensive use of Gesner elsewhere in his book makes it unnecessary and perhaps unlikely.

The borrowings of the passages concerning the preservation of gentles and the preparation of malt bait, on the other hand, seem to me to constitute clear evidence that Izaak Walton had seen and used the little book of 1577.[6] In themselves they are not of much significance, in spite of the hullabaloo that was raised about them in an astonishing number of newspaper stories, editorials, and letters in December 1956 when the facsimile of *The Arte of Angling* first appeared. Walton and all the other angling writers borrowed from their predecessors, just as non-angling writers did, and the fact that he neglected to mention this author, though he did give credit to Dennys,

---

[6] Walton was not alone among the angling writers in making use of the anonymous *Arte of Angling*. For example, on B_{v11}-B_{v11} of the little book are set forth thirteen numbered "gyftes" of the angler; they have nothing in common with the list of six charges which Dame Juliana lays on noble fishermen, but appear to be original with *The Arte of Angling*. In *The Secrets of Angling*, 1613, John Dennys in his section called *"The qualities of an Angler"* (D_4-D_7) followed them item for item, only transposing numbers seven and eight and omitting number twelve; usually he devoted a stanza to each of the "gyftes." In 1614 Markham repeated the same list, only substituting Prudence and Thankfulness for Prayer and Knowledge, but Markham was probably following Dennys, as he so often did.

Mascall, Markham, and Barker, may be disappointing, but it is not very remarkable.

What seems to me much more significant about the little book than the passages that Walton borrowed, is its plan. In structure it is a dialogue between Piscator and his friend Viator, whom he meets by chance and keeps with him for a day of fishing and later of fish eating and two sessions of fish talk at Piscator's house. Most of the dialogue consists of Piscator's explanation of the art of fishing and the habits of fish, explanations elicited by the questions of Viator, who becomes his pupil. The fish they catch are cooked by Piscator's wife, Cisley, who comments (somewhat unfavorably) on the life and hazards of fishermen, thus providing a pleasant variation to the fishing treatise.

If this description of the basic structure of *The Arte of Angling* sounds familiar, it is not surprising. The general plan of a dialogue between Piscator and Viator, whom he meets by chance and instructs in the art of fishing, sometimes by the stream and sometimes at the table as they eat their catch, which was Walton's most striking divergence from the six previously known English fishing books—this general plan is identical in *The Arte of Angling* and the first edition of *The Compleat Angler*. Even the names of the principals are the same, though Walton changed Viator to Venator and added Auceps in his later editions.

Clearly Walton took the general plan and structure of *The Arte of Angling* for his famous book; he took from it the names of the two principal characters in his first edition; and he also took, almost verbatim, his instructions for the cultivation of gentles and the preparation of malt bait. Like other writers of genius, Walton transformed what he borrowed. The anonymous author of *The Arte of Angling* had little of Walton's discursive charm, and his book has none of the idyllic quality of *The Compleat Angler*, or of its effective allusiveness. Yet this unknown writer of 1577 was no plodder and no amateur. His book seems to me to be of higher literary quality than any of the other early angling books except Walton's.

It is no wonder that Walton was attracted to the excellent device of presenting a fishing manual through dialogue and impersonation, for he saw it very well developed in *The Arte of Angling*. Some of the dialogue is nicely calculated to exploit the tensions of clashing personalities for the straight exposition of the basic facts about fish and tackle. The author has had the sound idea of making the pupil (Viator) somewhat hasty and impatient of results, and the fisherman (Piscator) more steady, but slightly irascible under pressure. As the book opens, Piscator is already fishing beside a stream, but with no luck. Viator comes up to him, and, after peering into his empty fishing pail, says:

Why, here is nothing, not one fyn.

Pi. No not one eye truly.

Vi. But I praye you howe long haue you been here?

Pi. I haue beene here this houre, and haue not had one bit.

Vi. Howe commeth that to passe?

Pı. Well ynough.

Vı. Nay you should say il ynough, for if I
shoulde rise so earely and in such a whisteling cold morning, and stand an houre
by yᵉ water side with mine angle, and
catch not a fishe, no nor haue so muche
as one bit, they shoulde bite on the bridle,
for one of vs, I would giue them the bag,
and bid them adue, and also make my
reconing, that it had been il ynough with
me, (as I saide) and not well ynough.

These lines constitute the introduction of the
pupil to the teacher of fishing. The presentation
of the objections of the infidel to the sacred pastime of angling are set in an appropriate context,
and the way is prepared to entice him into the
joys and rituals of the mystery.

While Viator watches, Piscator begins to catch
fish. He lands two roach and a dace while Viator
gets more and more excited. Then comes the in-
evitable hitch, and in pushing his luck too hard,
Piscator loses a hook. Patiently he goes about
setting on another, but the delay is too much for
the fidgeting Viator. He fumes and fusses and
declares that if *he* were managing the sport, no
such delay would be tolerated. He would carry
on, even using a bent pin for a hook and a stick
for a rod. The devoted fisherman, disgusted at
this neophyte impatience, says to him:

> you speake according to your knowledge,
> I would you had such an angle here that
> you might trie your cunning, whilst I
> were setting on of my hook

Vı. So Would I, I woulde pull them vp I trow.

The Context

Pɪ. Or else you cannot tel. What bayt would ye
haue?

Vɪ. One of yours.

Pɪ. You should pardon me.

Vɪ. Then I wold dig vp a worm with my knife
here abouts, and put it on.

Pɪ. And how would you do for a flote?

Vɪ. Tushe, when I felt the fishe bite, then I
would pull, and throw her vp, or else I
would tie a litle rotten stick about my line.
Laugh you?

Pɪ. Why, you woulde make a sicke man to
laugh.

Slowly Viator is led round to the admission
that fishing, of all crafts, is the one he would like
to have taught him, but he fears that he is too
impatient. As they discuss the art of the angler,
Piscator hooks a big perch, and Viator, under
careful directions, helps to land him, receiving
instructions about the habits and anatomy of
perch as he works. With Viator thus confirmed in
his resolve to learn about fishing, they part, and
Piscator takes his catch home to his wife Cisley.

This, I submit, is a very skillful opening for a
fishing manual. The author has nicely created
the friction between the patient man and the
hasty man, between experience and inexperience,
to lead into his further exposition. What dramatist of the sixties or seventies did any better with
an opening scene?

Further on in his narrative the author adroitly
contrives another impediment to the steady flow
of the fishing lore. At dinner on the evening of
this first day, Cisley, Piscator's wife, interrupts
the fishing instruction to protest to Viator,

    I pray you sir, let my husband a while alone,
vntill he haue eaten, and then you can not
please him better at meat then to talke of
angling, though for my part I would he
had neuer knowen what angling ment.

Vi. Why I pray you?

Ci. I thinke he had neuer known what the
colicke had ment, if he had not known
what angling had ment.

Vi. Is it euen so?

Pi. Soft dame.

Vi. Nay, I pray you let vs two alone, and eate
you a while, for I beleeue that your wife
is not fasting no more than I: now mistresse, is it true that your husbāde hath
caught the collicke with fishing?

Ci. Surely I suppose so, with his long standing,
long fasting, & coldenesse of his feete, yea
and sometimes sitting on the cold ground:
for all is one to him, whether he catch or
not catch: yea and sometimes he cōmeth
home with the collick in deed, and is not
wel of two or three dayes after, so that I
hope he will giue it ouer shortly.

Vi. Is this true?

Pi. Yea, what then?

This exchange puts Viator off, and Piscator
must have taken several speeches to defend angling from the wifely objections of Cisley, but at
this point two leaves of the book are missing.
How he upheld his pastime we cannot tell, but
it was a successful defence, for after the break
Viator's eagerness has been renewed and Piscator
is in full cry explaining the intricacies of fishing
from a boat.

The Context

And so the instruction goes on, with disquisitions on the ruffe, the perch, the pickerel, the chub, the pike, the carp, the bream, the roach, and the dace. There are occasional interruptions from Cisley, who once says, "You men say that women bee talkatiue, but here is suche a number of words about nothing, as passeth."

Later on Viator comes again to Piscator's house for further talk, and finally the little book ends with Piscator's declaration, "It is time I were gone," and the completely converted Viator's enthusiastic reply, "Wel, if you hie you not apace, I wilbe at the Riuer before you."

There is always a temptation to exaggerate the value of the newly discovered, but it is obvious that *The Arte of Angling* will never supplant *The Compleat Angler* in popular or critical esteem. Its author, however, is no unlettered angler whose enthusiasm has led him to a halting exposition of his fishing lore; I think he understands dialogue better than Walton does, and his powers of characterization are more highly developed—at least in his secondary figures. In contriving his situations to elicit the exposition, he shows great skill; he is easy in the handling of a dramatic problem at which Walton is sometimes awkward. His Piscator does not have the charm or the depth of Walton's, but his pupil seems to me to be more fully realized than Viator-Venator. His assurance in dialogue and characterization persuade me that he was not an inexperienced writer.

This author's skill and his new prominence in the genealogy of English fishing books make his anonymity all the more challenging—at least to me. The contents of the book will not quite serve to identify him, but they furnish several clues which ought to help. One must assume, if these various bits of evidence are to be accepted as clues to the identity of the author, that the writer of *The Arte of Angling* made Piscator reflect his own experience, as Walton in *The Compleat Angler* made *his* Piscator reflect *his* experience.[7]

Now if *The Arte of Angling* were pure fiction, such an assumption of the identification of the author with the principal character would provide a very dangerous trap, the trap into which Shakespearean critics have been so happily tumbling for generations. But *The Arte of Angling* is a manual, not pure fiction. And a manual is written for the purpose of making the practical experience of the author available to the reader. In these circumstances I should be inclined to accept the assumption that the places Piscator

[7] If, in an analogous situation, *The Compleat Angler* were anonymous, Izaak Walton could have been identified through the places and the friends Piscator mentions in the edition of 1653: "I have stretch'd my legs up Totnam Hill" (B_1); "As we walk and fish toward *London* to morrow" (P_3); "as we go toward *London*" (P_6^v); "Charles Brandon (neer to the *Swan* in *Golding-Lane*): or to Mr Fletcher in the Court . . . hard by the west end of Saint *Pauls* Church" (Q_2); "we shal be at Totenham *High-Cross*" (Q_3); "a river not far from Canterbury" (N_6^v); "(as Winchester or the Thames about Windsor) . . . (in both which places I have caught . . .)" (G_3); "Henry Wotton (a man with whom I have often fished and conversed)" (C_8^v, also O_7^v, Q_1^v-Q_2); "honest Sir George Hastings . . . has told me" (G_3^v, also K_6^v and Q_1^v-Q_2); "a song . . . made at my request by Mr. *William Basse*" (F_5^v); "I have been a fishing with old Oliver Henly" (K_5^v), and the like.

mentions in *The Arte of Angling* are the places the author had visited, just as Piscator's experience with live minnows is the author's experience. There is a danger of pushing this assumption too far, but it may be useful for a start toward identifying the author.

To begin with, the specific places mentioned by the author are on the Ouse, downstream from Buckinghamshire and Bedfordshire, in or near "our fennes." He refers to the stream as "oure Riuer, called the Ouse," a phrasing that would seem to indicate not only that he fished the Ouse but that long residence gave him the usual local sense of possession.

A story that Piscator tells about the range of a bream in the Ouse brings us a little closer to his particular part of it. The anecdote concerns a certain fish that he bought when it was caught in a net "in drawing the water at Huntington bridge." Piscator shows that he was present when the fish was taken, for he says "shee was a very great fishe, of a breame, bothe in bredth and thicknesse, as euer I sawe." Like most such fish, this one got away, "whiche," says Piscator, "grieued mee somewhat."

But this fish story has a happier ending than most. Piscator says that "within three or foure dayes afterwarde the water beneathe vs also was drawne at a towne called saint Tyues, three myle from vs by land, but foure good mile by water, and there was that self same breame taken again." And he continues, "so I was faine to bye her the second time," again indicating that he was present at Huntingdon Bridge when the bream was taken the first time. At the taking at St. Ives he must also have been present, or perhaps he was only known to the fishermen who took her the second time and who graciously accepted a second payment from him. In either case he must have been present in the vicinity over a period of several days, and familiar with it. One of his phrases in this story indicates residence in the neighborhood, for he says that St. Ives is three miles "from vs" by land. Another phrase brings us still closer to his residence. When he speaks of the draining of the river at St. Ives, he says that "the water beneathe vs also was drawne at a towne called saint Tyues," which I take to mean that he lived upstream from that town. Taken together, these various phrases seem to indicate that the author of *The Arte of Angling* lived either in the town of Huntingdon or a mile or two downstream from it.

Another story in the book reveals a former residence of the author. When he is instructing his pupil Viator about the habits of chevin, Piscator says,

> . . . when I dwelled in Sauoye, the ouermost parts of Switzerlande, in angling in a part of Losana lake, & the ditch of Geneua, but chiefly in ye swift Rodanus, I tooke sometime the Cheuin and very faire.

If Piscator was English and was living in or near Geneva several years before 1577 when his angling book was published, why was he there? One phrase later in this passage offers a faint suggestion. He says that the local inhabitants who watched him fishing in or near Geneva "marueled that I, or any of my countrimen" would eat the chevin. "Any of my countrimen" suggests that other English folk were with him and also known to eat the fish. An English group or colony living in the vicinity of Geneva before 1577—say from ten to thirty years before—suggests the Marian exiles. Of course there were English other than the Marian exiles in Geneva between about 1547 and 1567, but these exiles seem to me, at the moment, to provide the most likely hiding place for this author.

It might be further remarked that, though *The Arte of Angling* as a whole is not notably pious, the tutorial of fishing teacher and fishing pupil which begins when Viator comes to supper at Piscator's house is quite compatible with the hypothesis that Piscator was a Marian exile. After four or five short exchanges, Viator asks Piscator to begin with the antiquity of angling—the aspect of the sport with which, incidentally, Dennys, Markham, and Walton also begin. Piscator refuses, and introduces angling in his own way by a five or six-page theological disquisition which places angling in its proper context in God's universe. I suppose that Elizabethans of various persuasions might have insisted on such an introduction, but it seems to me at least suitable for a returned Marian exile.

There is one other slight clue in the text which might serve as a guide in the author search. Near the end of the book Piscator says in response to Viator's question about trout fishing:

The Arte of Angling

I dare not well deale in y^e angling of y^e
Trout, for displesing of one of our wardens,
which either is coūted the best trouter in
England, or so thinketh, who would not (as
I suppose) haue the taking of that fish common, but yet thus muche I may say, that
he worketh with a flie in a boxe. (E$_{vii}$^{v})

Ignoring the intriguing "flie in a boxe," notice the "one of our wardens." It suggests a warden for some group with which Piscator, and
possibly Viator also, was closely associated. What
kind of a warden? A guild warden? The warden
of a college, or hospital, or alms house? A church
warden? The warden of a grammar school?

In summary, then, I should guess the author
of *The Arte of Angling*, 1577, to have been: (a)
a returned Marian exile who had lived in or
near Geneva; (b) an inhabitant of, or a frequent
visitor in, the county of Huntingdon, either in
the town of Huntingdon itself, or a mile or two
down the Ouse toward St. Ives; (c) a man with
some close association with a guild, college,
church, hospital, alms house, or grammar school
whose warden, also a fisherman, sometimes
troubled him; (d) a man who had published
other works, for the author seems to me much too
skillful in the presentation of his material and
characters to have been an inexperienced writer.
(It would be pleasant for me to imagine that his
skill in character development, dialogue, and
character oppositions came from play writing,
but other Elizabethans could write dialogue, and
Marian exiles and leisurely fishermen do not sug-

gest the playwright pattern.) (e) an experienced and enthusiastic angler.

I wish I could show that the object of this search was the loved and respected Alexander Nowell (1507?-1602), Dean of St. Pauls,[8] who prepared the catechism. Nowell was widely known as an angler. His portrait at Brasenose College, Oxford, shows him with his fishing tackle. Izaak Walton speaks in the warmest terms of his character and his long devotion to angling.[9] The Bishop of London granted to Nowell very special fishing rights in his parish of Great Hadham in Hertfordshire. He had been a Marian

[8] See Ralph Churton, *The Life of Alexander Nowell, Dean of St. Pauls.* Oxford, 1809.

[9] 1653 edition, C_7-C_8^v. Evidently Walton thought Dean Nowell one of the better examples of the fine character of the fisherman. In his second edition, that of 1655, he expanded his account of Nowell to include a description of his portrait with the fishing tackle in Brasenose College. In the third edition of 1661 he expanded the account still further to include the inscription on the portrait. Incidentally, the portrait of Dean Nowell which now hangs in the Hall at Brasenose, though it shows several fish hooks and a fishing rod, lacks other details described by Walton. My investigation at the National Portrait Gallery Library in London of the records and descriptions of Nowell portraits makes it appear most likely that the portrait now at Brasenose really is the one Walton saw, but that his memory tricked him into inventing a few more bits of fishing tackle than he had really seen. John Buchan in his book on Brasenose College describes several of the portraits in the Hall, singling out the Nowell portrait as his favorite. (*Brasenose College,* London, 1898. pp. 87-8) Instead of describing it himself, he admiringly quotes Walton's description from *The Compleat Angler,* not noting in his enthusiasm that Walton has added a little extra fishing tackle.

exile. He was very active in the refounding and developing of a grammar school with a warden. He had much literary experience. He is just the sort of candidate I want to urge. But alas, his fishing rivers were the Thames and the Ash, not, so far as we know, the Ouse. His grammar school was near Manchester; his favorite retreat was in Hertfordshire, and I cannot associate him in any way with Huntingdon. Even as a Marian exile he seems to have lived principally in Frankfort, not Geneva.[10]

But the fact that Alexander Nowell so nearly fits the shadow of the angling author in this anonymous book encourages me to think that the shadow I have outlined is not a grotesque or impossible one. Perhaps someone with greater experience than mine in the records of the Marian exiles and in the local histories of Huntingdonshire will be able to produce the unknown author whose graceful exposition of his cherished pastime provided a seminal book in English angling literature.

GERALD EADES BENTLEY

[10] Churton, *op. cit.*, passim.

The Arte of Angling

Facsimile

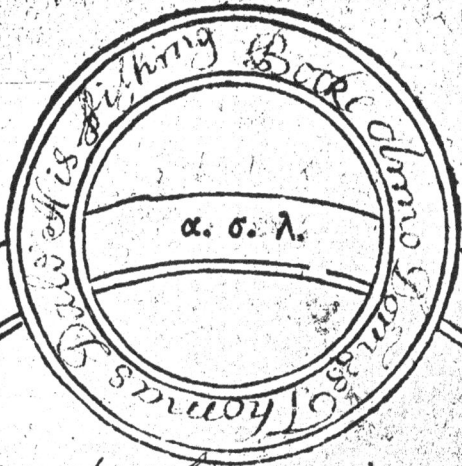

α. σ. λ.

Eli Balkers Fishing Book
Stoke on trent Staffordshire
Septr 1841

Januarÿ   1 January
Februarÿ   2 February
maert   3 Marsh
aprill   4 Aprill
maÿ   5 May
junÿ   6 June
julÿ   7 July
Augu(st)   8 August
September   9 September
october   10 October
november   11 November
december   12 December
these are ÿ 12 monthes in the
year

A dialogue betweene
Viator and Piscator.

What friende Piscator, are you euen at it so early?

Piscator. Yea, the prouerb is truly in me verified. Early vp and neuer the neere, al the speede is in the morning.

Ui. Is it euen so? May I bee so bolde as to looke into your paile?

Pi. Yea hardily.

Ui. Why, here is nothing, not one fyn.

Pi. Not one eye truly.

Ui. But I praye you howe long haue you been here?

Pi. I haue beene here this houre, and haue not had one bit.

Ui. Howe commeth that to passe?

Pi. Well ynough.

Ui. Nay you should say il ynough.

for if I shoulde rise so early and in such a whisteling cold morning, and stand an houre by $\bar{y}$ water side with mine angle, and catch not a fishe, no nor haue so muche as one bit, they shoulde bite on the bridle, for one of vs, I would giue them the bag, and bid them adue, and also make my reconing, that it had been il ynough with me, (as I saide) and not well ynough.

Pi. Yea sir, when I saide, well ynough, I did not meane of my not taking of fish, but that it might well ynough be, by a reason two or three to render the cause, or causes of their not biting.

Vi. And doe you intend to tarrie vntil those causes be ouer?

Pi. I wil not say so, but I intend to trie one houre longer, by Gods grace, and then if they bite not, farewell they.

Vi.

Vi. Say you so? may a man take
a stoole, and sit down on the ground
by you, vntil that houre be ouer?

Pi. Yea, so that you sitte not ouer
neere the water.

Vi. Nay I trow, I will sitte farre
inough off for slipping in.

Pi. I do not meane therefore, but
I wold not haue you sit, so that the
fishe may see either your shaddowe,
your face, or any part of you.

Vi. And why? are they so quicke
of sight?

Pi. Looke what they lacke in hearing, it is supplied vnto them in seeing chiefly, and also in feeling, and
tasting, therefore with the least mouing, they shun straight vnlesse it be
the Pikerell.

Vi. Well, now I am sette, may I
then talke, and not hinder your fishing?

Pi. Spare not, but not to loude?

Vi. Do the fiſhe then heare?

Pi. No, you may talke, hoope oʒ
hollowe, and neuer ſtirre them, but
I woulde not gladly by your loude
talking, that either ſome bungler,
idle perſon, oʒ ieſter, might thereby,
reſoʒt vnto vs, and alſo I know not
what you haue to ſay, foʒ freends as
they ſeldome meete, ſo ſpare they not
to vtter ſecretes, which loude talke
doth oftentimes hurt, and the truth
is, the water hathe an Eccho, moʒe
than the land, and therefoʒe eaſelier
heard : Now, what haue you to ſay?

Vi. Oh, there was a bit.

Pi. Yea and a bit.

Vi. Why, haue you her?

Pi. Nay not yet, but I hope to
haue, loe, howe ſay you? now I haue
her in deede.

Vi. Surely wel ſaide, now of like
the ſpoʒt doth begin. O caſt in again
foʒ an other.

Pi.

Pi. So wil J, & doubt you not my freend Uiator, but you shal see sport.

Ui. How knowe you?

Pi. Naye softe there, but tell mee anon, whither J saide true or no: Nowe a Gods name, haue among thē, you shall see another bit straight way, & mark whē my floate is in the same place that J had my laſt bit in.

Ui. Why?

Pi. Ther shal you see the bit again.

Ui. Now it is at the place almoſt, now, there is a bit in deede, wel ſtriken, ye haue het againe.

Pi. J shal haue by and by, J hope.

Ui. Up with her man.

Pi. No haſt but good, it is a good fish.

Ui. Therefore if your angle were in my hand, J would make the more haſt, and toſſe her vp, ouer my head.

Pi. Haſt in deede might ſo make waſt, lo here ſhe is nowe.

A.iii.

Ui.

Ui. Surely it is a trimme fishe, I
pray you lay in again, for I see now
here wilbe sport in deede.

Pi. I will. I haue spied a faulte,
which I had neede to mend, but you
are so haftie.

Ui. Tush mend your faults soone
as most do, and plie your sport, so lo,
now another bite by and by I warrant you.

Pi. I hope so.

Ui. Strike.

Pi. I warrant you, let me alone,
if I misse a bite tel me.

Ui. You haue her againe.

Pi. God sende her me, for it is a
good fish, and a Dace, I beleeue.

Ui. Why what are the other two?

Pi. Roches.

Ui. Can you tel before you see her,
what kinde of fish it is?

Pi. I haue a gesse, I tolde you it
was a Dace.

Ui.

Vi. In deede nowe you haue her, your gesse was a true gesse belike, & I must needs say, it is another kind I see by her making and colour, for she is rounder & whiter. Ho w nowe? Why lay you not in againe?

Pi. Nay, now I wil sit downe by you a while and mend a fault.

Vi. I pray you caste in once more for my pleasure.

Pi. What and I leese my hooke?

Vi. Farewel it, there is but a hook lost.

Pi. Yea friende, a good hooke is not so sone foūd againe, but to pleasure you, there it is, and you shall see me lose it straight.

Vi. I warrant you for an egge at Easter.

Pi. Your warrant is as good, as an obligation sealed with butter.

Vi. There was a faire bite.

Pi. You say true, and a foule hit,

for

for all is loste, thus it is to be ruled
by you,it is maruel if all be not gon,
I had warning, I might haue take
heede,there is a hooke gone,nowe I
must sit downe with losse.

    Ui. I am sorie nowe that you sat
not downe afore. Haue you any mo
hookes here:

    Pi. Yea I trow,or else I were but
a simple fisher, if I had not store of
hookes about mee, I might put vp
pipes.

    Ui. Howe will you do to set it on:
haue you any thred about you:

    Pi. You are a wise man, doe you
thinke that Anglers deuise to set on
their hookes with thread:

    Ui. Why not,and make a hook of
a bowed pinne, and an Angle of
a sticke.

    Pi. Like workman,like foole, you
speake according to your knowlege,
I would you had such an angle here
                    that

that you might trie your cunning,
whilst I were setting on of my hook

Vi. So would I, I woulde pull
them vp I trow.

Pi. Oz else you cannot tel. What
bayt would ye haue?

Vi. One of yours.

Pi. You should pardon me.

Vi. Then I wold dig vp a wozm
with my knife here abouts, and put
it on.

Pi. And how would you do foz a
flote?

Vi. Tushe, when I felt the fishe
bite, then I would pull, and thzow
her vp, oz else I would tie a litle rotten stick about my line. Laugh you?

Pi. Why, you woulde make a sicke
man to laugh.

Vi. Now surely lend me but a fa-
dome of thzead, and you shall see me
an Angler straight.

Pi. What so soone?

A.v.   Vi

Ui. Yea for I haue a pin,& I will cut a wand out of this willowehere by,and dig vp a worme as I saide, if you wil not lend me a bait,and catch some or euer you be readie, you sit so long fidling about tying on of your hooke.

Pi. So then you wold haue your rod,your line,your hooke,your bait, and your fish, or euer I were readie to lay in again:but good sir,wher be your plumbets and your plumb?

Ui. Nay then we shall neuer haue done,the bait wil sinke of it self with the waight of the pin,and as for the plumb,I cannot tel what it means.

Pi. I thinke so,nor shal not at my hand. And where is your meate?

Ui. Meate qd ye, they shal be my meat when I haue catched them.

Pi. Wel said,that was wel put to.

Ui. Say you so,vp I wil for it,and prepare my selfe.

Pi.

Pi. Tush, tush, I pray you sit stil,
for now you do no harme, you were
as good sit stil for naught as rise for
naught: I tooke losse euen nowe at
your request, either take ye no harme
or do none at my request.

Vi. Now you make me to laughe,
you are afraide that I should kil thē
vp before you be readie.

Pi. If you had alreadie that you
speak off, where is the beard of your
hooke?

Vi. I tell you, they shoulde neuer
haue leasure to slipp off; I would so
fling them to land.

Pi. Why, is there no more vse to
the beard belonging, but to holde on
the fish?

Vi. Not that I knowe, is there?

Pi. Nay soft, you came not where
it grew, you speak in deed according
to your knowlege. Now am I redy.

Vi. It is time I trow, I pray you
let

let me see howe you haue tied it on.

Pi. Tied it on, howe rightly you haue your termes.

Ui. Howe then? bound it on?

Pi. Euen which you will.

Ui. Oh so fine you be, there is no occupation I perceiue, but ther is a glozie in it.

Pi. So, so, it will be a good while oz euer you be a good fisher.

Ui. Why?

Pi. You do but iest at it, and therfoze I see wel that you minde not to learne to angle.

Ui. Yes truly, of all crafts I wold most gladly haue it taught mee, but foz one thing: ⁊ that is, I loue not to stand, as I perceiue that you doe sometime an whole houre, and take not a fish, foz they must bite straight way with me, oz I am gon: foz who would stand gazing on the water so long, and haue no spozt, it is but te=

dious

dious idleneſſe, yea and ſometimes a wet ſkin, yea head & all if his foote ſlip: and in a colde mozning he may catch that in his feete, that will not out of his head a good while after, & I thinke it is not very good foz the collike.

Pi. Then it is wel that ye know no moze of it, ſeeing that you can tell of ſo many diſcōmodities, that doth belong vnto it, but what if a man cā tell you howe not onely to auoide all theſe, but alſo to haue twiſe ſo many commodities by it, if he once knowe the Art thozowly.

Ui. There are my fozenamed two termes mended. I ſee wel, that angling is neither an occupation, noz a craft, but an art, and not without ſome ſkil: foz I doe in deede ſuppoſe, that he which maketh an occupatiō of it, may oftē eat his bzead dzie, yea & perhaps bzing him to beg it, but

I do

I do thinke that you doe vse it in the best kinde, and ý is for recreation, for pastime, and sometimes to get you a stomach.

Pi. It may be vsed of sundrie men to sundrie endes, and of the cunning man, to all those ends that are lawfull.

Vi. But how now, al this while and not a fishe? this I like not, the bite is done, I thought you tarried too long or euer you threwe in your bait againe, or else my talke, though as you say, that it trouble not the fish, yet it may be that it hath troubled you, so that you tende not so well to your fishing, as you did before you were moued.

Pi. In deede I could be wel content to haue lesse talk now, my messe of fishe beeing so litle, that I might the more attentiuely take heede, for I haue lost a bite or two that you
                                                    sawe

saw not, and some that I did not see,
noz you neither, vntil it was past, besides some practises that belongeth
to this science, that nowe I woulde
put in vze if you were not here, to
make vp my dish of fishe withall oz
euer I went, oz else it shoulde goe
hard.

Vi. Why then I perceiue I am
now a let vnto you, but I hope you
be not angrie, foz surely I ment nothing but mirth, notwithstanding,
I will trouble you no longer, but
leaue you where I founde you, and
S. Peters master be with you, pzay-
ing you not to be offended, foz I perceiue the fisherman may sometimes
be displeased, as well as haukers oz
hunters.

Pi. Nay truly, but I must needes
tell you, that we be not altogethers
voide of passions, and choler, yet assure your self, as you came my frend,
so

so shall you go on my behalfe, & that shall ye well knowe, if you will come to me soone to supper, and then shall ye be a partaker, not onely at my table of my dayes worke, but also, if you intreat me faire, & bring a quart of sacke with you, and minde in deed to be acquainted in our ministerie, & to know the mysteries of it, you shall be welcome: and I pray you come.

Vi. I thāk you, I wil not fayl god willing. God be wō you vntill soone, now vse your knacks, for I am gon.

Pi. Come againe I pray you, and helpe me with your hand a litle, for I haue nowe neede of your help, I haue striken a good fish, and shal not I feare me, be able to land hir alone.

Vi. It is a greate one in deede by the bending of your angle. What fish is it trowe you.

Pi. A pearche, it shoulde be, by the grosenes of the bite, and by the hardnesse

nesse of the stroke & his swattering.

Ui. Giue me your angle, and take you him vppe when he comes to the banke side.

Pi. Nay not so, for so wee might loose him, for the guiding of the line is one of the best feats when a good fish is stroken : it is a Perch in deed, & that a faire one , God send vs well to land him, hee will mend our dish well, see howe he gapes, stares, and holds vp his bristles , I must pray you to lie downe flat on your belly, & hold faste by the ground with your one hand, or else let me tread on the skirts of your coat with my left foote that you slip not in, and take him vp with your other hande , for I will with my line leade him harde to the bank, for now he is tired.

Ui. Yea but howe shall I deale with him for his pricks, for he hathe more than you see?

B.   Pisc.

Pi. Put your finger vnder his
throte, vnder one of his gilles into
his mouth, I meane your forefinger
and your thumb into his mouthe, &
so your finger and your thumb meeting in his mouthe, holde them fast
together, and so throw him vp lustily to land, for that line & those hooks
wil not breake.

Vi. He will bite me.

Pi. No I warrant you, doe as
I bid you, he hathe no teethe in his
mouth, they be downe in his throte.

Vi. How shall we now do, he holdeth his chaps together as hard as
may be?

Pi. Take him harde by the nape
of the necke, and so bring him vp.

Vi. I wil, I haue him nowe.

Pi. Holde fast whilst I lay down
mine angle and help you vp, bicause
you haue but one hand, so, well said,
now we haue him.

Vi.

Wi. Surely, surely, it is a good
fish, how would you haue done if I
had not been here? I perceiue now,
that it is meete for you to haue one
with you: what haue we there? what
but one haire? why that passeth.

Pi. No in deed, for I came to day
to this plat a Roching, & therefore
brought but my Roch gieres, & like
a wise man, left one of my tooles at
home for hast, whiche if I had brought, I could haue landed him without your help.

Wi. I pray you be not without
your shift, and all to driue me away,
well, fare you well now in deed.

Pi. God be with you, & I thanke
you for your paines.

Piscator and his wife Cisley.

Ow nowe wife, is the brothe
ready.

Cisley. In deede I haue had

good

good leyfure : good Lord hufbande
where haue you beene all this daye,
haue you dined?

Pi. No truly, my firft bread is yet
to eate fithens you fawe me, therfore
let my fupper bee readie as foone as
may be.

Ci. So will J, but what haue you
brought?

Pi. Fetche me a platter and you
fhall fee.

Ci. Here is one fhal J take them
out?

Pi. No Dame, J will take them
out, & lay euery fort by them felues.
How fay you Cilley, is there not a
good difh?

Ci. J am gladde now that J did
throw an olde fhooe after you in the
morning, here is a meffe in deede.

Pi. Your old fhooe was fit for an
old foolifh woman to haue throwen,
that hathe more confidence in fuch
Difmole

diſmole toies than in the prouidence
of God,who guideth aſwel the fiſhes
in the ſea, as the foules in the ayre,
but I knowe you ſpeake merrily as
I did when I bad you do it.

Ci. How will you haue them dreſſed,for as here be many ſorts,ſo may
you haue them dreſſed after ſundrie
manners.

Pi. Let them I pray you be ordered after the beſt manner, for my
freend Uiator wilbe here at ſupper.

Ci. They ſhall.

Uiator. Ho, God be here.

Pi. Dare you come, come neere,
I know you by your voice.

Ui. Ah,you are come howe I perceiue.

Pi. Now ſurely you are welcom,
what, and your ſack too: that is ho-
neſtly ſaid: Is it good ſack:

Ui. I can not tel,for of all wines
B.iii.   I

I loue it not,therfore I did not say.

Pi. And why? do you knowe any thing by it?

Ui. Yea Piscator, I haue seene such liuely fellows,shozt with sharp heads,as they say that somtime you fish withal, powzed out into a goblet,foz whē the wine hath bin dzunk there haue they lien.

Pi. Tush, if you wil neither eate noz dzinke of any thing that quicke cattel is in,oz wil bzede in,you will hardly holde them in your mouthe while you angle,that they may bee the readier to put on your hooke.

Ui. Out vpon it, and if I wiste that that were of necessitie, I wold ether angle in those moneths when they be out of season, oz else with some other baits as good, oz not at all.

Pi. Well sit downe I pzay you, our supper will come in by and by,
we

we will haue one fit at fiſhing vntill meate come.

Ui. Why then I praye you let vs knowe ſome what of the antiquitie of it.

Pi. Nay let me rather make mine introduction to the matter, and ſo come to that afterward. Firſt you muſt vnderſtande, that as God did make all thinges for man, ſo ſhoulde he haue had a great deale of more cō modious pleaſure in his creatures than he hath, had he not by his diſo bedience made them bothe diſobedi ent & hurtful, yea I do ſuppoſe that neither the heauens, or any powers aboue, nether the earth or any thing therin, either could or woulde haue hurt man, if man had not firſt hurte himſelfe. And alſo the huge ſea, with all the benefits therof, and al others of waters as meares, lakes, ponds, riuers, and ſtreames, ſhould haue

B.iiii.   giuen

giuen their goodes and riches vnto
man, if man had not giuen himselfe
to sinne, & so to Sathan: By which
meanes he hath not onely lost as I
said (and so all we that come of him)
infinite commodities, but also those
that he hathe, he must winne them
with great care and sore labour, and
with all deuise, policie, and art that
he can, sometime not without the
perill of his life: for there is not the
smallest fish that is, that is not now
to good for a man, hauing streame
at wil, without his greate industrie
to catche her.

  Vi. Why then if earthly thinges
are so hard to come by, by the reason
of our former fathers fall, howe are
we able to come by heauenly things
that are beyond our labour? I suppose that we are farre weaker that
way.

  Pi. It is true, for he that saide In
sudore

sudore vultus tui.&c. In y̆ sweat of thy
browes thou shalt get thy liuing, &
that the earth shoulde beare nought
but brambles and briers, and that
as man came from earth, so to earth
he shoulde returne: did not say that
man in his labours should get hea-
uen, but onely the winning of hea-
uen he left to one that neuer fell,and
so by him, to haue it, and all other
good thinges also, Christe Iesus I
meane.

Vi. Well,nowe to your matter a-
gaine.

Pi. To returne yet for all that,
the same almightie God hathe not so
auenged the fall and offence of man,
that hee shoulde be altogether ouer
pressed with carefull trauayle, but
hathe spiced mans paines with delight,pastime, and recreation many
waies, in the finding, winning, or
ending of his labours, whereof the

B.v.   fisher

fisher, faulconer, and hunter are well
able to report. And as the same al=
mightie, hathe not made al kinde of
liuing creatures vpon earthe, to bee
but one, but diuided them into bea=
stes, foules, fishes, and wormes, and
they of diuers sortes in euery kind,
so hath he giuen to sundrie men, sun=
drie mindes, some in this, and some
in that to haue pleasure : for if all
his liuing Creatures shoulde haue
beene of one sorte, as all fishes, all
beastes, or al foules, so had lothsom=
nesse & wast, hurt appetite and plea=
sure, But now to speake more perti=
cularly and to our purpose. As in fi=
shing, fouling, and hunting, there
is degrees bothe of costes, paines,
pleasures, and profits, so what cost
paine, pleasure, or profite, the hun=
ter or hauker hath, as I am not skil=
full in either of them, so do I leaue
such as would know to the sundrie
                              bookes

books set out by sundrie men, and in
sundrie tongues, that doth write of
them bothe at large : neither doe I
purpose so to speake vnto you of fishing as seueraly to tel of al the cost,
paine, pleasure, or profit, that is in
that maruelous and woonderfull
science.

Vi. No freend Piscator, I come
not therefore, only I pray you speak
of angling.

Pi. So I will, as of that pleasure that I haue alwayes moste recreated my self withal, and had most
delight in, and is moste meetest for a
solitary mã, and is also of light cost:
yet do I not intend to make my selfe
so skilfull vnto you in the Art of angling, as to leaue out nothing that
might be said, no more than you shal
find me to contemn that which hath
ben put in print heretofore: for this
I know, that both time, place, kind,
                                    and

and cuſtome, is not ſo knowen vnto
me; but that I may want in any of
ẙ foure, yea & in al, to ſay that may be
ſaide. But what I do knowe by re-
poꝛt, by reading oꝛ by experience, by
my ſelf at home oꝛ abꝛode, I wil god
willing not hide it from you, and if
you can learne moꝛe of any others,
oꝛ that at this time I ſhal foꝛget oꝛ
hereafter find any moꝛe knowledge,
take that foꝛ aduantage. And this
I tel you plaine, that the couetous,
& greedie man (foꝛ auoiding ſpoyle)
may not be allowed in this fellow-
ſhip, neither may the ſluggerd ſlee-
py ſlouen, be ſeene in this ſcience:
neither the pooꝛe man, leaſt it make
him pooꝛer, and beg his bꝛead to his
fiſh: the angrie man alſo and the fear
full man, with the buſie bodie, muſt
tarie at home, & rather hut oꝛ hauke.
  Ui. Why then I pꝛay you, what
gyftes muſt he haue that ſhal be of
youꝛ

your companie.

Pi. 1 He must haue faith, beleeuing
that there is fish where he commeth
to angle. 2. He must haue hope that
they wil bite. 3. Loue to the owner
of the game. 4. Also patience if they
wil not bite, or any mishap come, by
leasing of fishe, hooke, or otherwise.
5. Humilitie to stoupe, if neede be to
kneele, or lie downe on his belly, as
you did to day. 6. Fortitude, with
manly corage, to deale with the biggest that commeth. 7. Knowledge
adioyned to wisedome, to deuise all
manner of waies how to make them
bite, and to finde the fault. 8. Libera-
litie in feeding of them. 9. A content
mind with a sufficient messe, yea and
though you goe home without. 10.

Also he must vse prayer, knowing
that it is God that doth bring bothe
foule to the net, & fishe to the bayte.
11 Fasting he may not bee offended
with

withall, but acquaint himselfe with
it, if it be from morning vntil night,
to abide and seeke for the bit. 12 Also
he must do almes deedes : that is to
say, if he meete a sickly pooze body, oz
doth knowe any suche in the parish,
that woulde be glad of a fewe fishes
to make a litle broth with all (as often times is desired of sicke persons)
then he may not sticke to send them
some, oz altogether. And if he haue
none, yet with all diligence that may
be, trie with his angle to get some
for the diseased person. 13 The last
point of all the inward gifts ψ doth
belóg to an angler is memozie, that
is, that he forget nothing at home,
when he setteth out, noz any thing
behind him at his returne.

   Vi. Why man, if he haue an angle
and baits, what need any moze: and
a small memozie will serue for those
two.

Pi.

of Angling.

Pi. You must take ii. swans quils, one quil must be greater than another, and cut off both the stopped endes, and then put the one cut end into the other as hard as you can for cleauing of the vttermost, that they may be close for taking of water, & look that they haue no holes in the smaller ends, and that quil that is within the other, let that bee lowest in the water. Then must you take an other swans quill, and cut it in two such pieces as may be put on eache end of your flote one, so that thends of your double quil or flote appeare out when your line is put thorowe those two peeces , as for exam= ple here is one readie made,

Here must we stay, now is sup= per come,

Vi. I am the more sorie, for
your

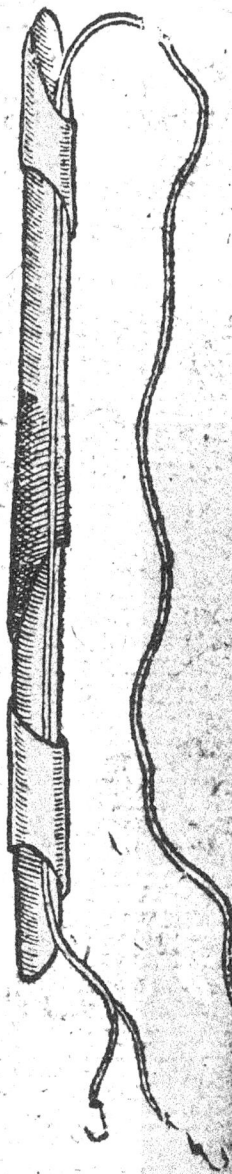

your talke is meat and dꝛink to me.

Pi. Yea, but meate and dꝛinke is fitter foꝛ me , that haue not eaten to Day. Well, let vs haue grace.

Ui. Haue ye not a fiſh grace?

Pi. Yes, that I haue, and that foꝛ an angler.

> Almightie God, that theſe did make,
>   As ſaith his holy book:
> And gaue me cunning them to take,
>   And brought them to my hooke.
> To him be praiſe for euermore,
>   That daily doth vs feede :
> And doth increaſe by ſpaun ſuche ſtore,
>   To ſerue vs at our neede.

Ui. A very good grace and a fitt : Nowe I pꝛay you lette your Ciſley come in.

Pi. Call your mother in, maide.

Ui. What fiſh call you theſe?

Pi. Goodgions

Ui. They be very good in deede, & wel

well dreſſed, how take you theſe?

Pi. Theſe are as fit for a yong be
ginner as may be, for one bait doth
ſerue them at all ſeaſons, & you may
make thē to bite al dai, if you haue ſū
drie places : Come wife come, thou
thinkeſt that nothing is well done,
vnleſſe thou be at the one ende of it :
ſit down and eat, for I am hungrie.

Ci. I beleeue well , howe like you
your broth?

Pi. Hunger findeth no fault.

Vi. But I pray you teache me to
kill theſe pleaſant fiſhes.

Ci. I pray you ſir, let my huſband
a while alone, vntill he haue eaten,
and then you can not pleaſe him better at meat then to talke of angling,
though for my part I would he had
neuer knowen what angling ment.

Vi. Why I pray you?

Ci. I thinke he had neuer known
what the colicke had ment, if he had

not known what angling had ment

Wi. Is it euen so?

Pi. Soft dame.

Wi. Nay, I pray you let vs two
alone, and eate you a while, for I beleeue that your wife is not fasting
no moze than I: now mistresse, is it
true that your husbáde hath caught
the collicke with fishing?

Ci. Surely I suppose so, with his
long standing, long fasting, & coldenesse of his feete, yea and some times
sitting on the cold ground: for all is
one to him, whether he catch oz not
catch: yea and somtimes he cómeth
home with the collick in deed, and is
not wel of two oz three dayes after,
so that I hope he will giue it ouer
shortly.

Wi. Is this true?

Pi. Yea, what then?

Wi. Then I say, Fælix quem faciunt aliena pericula cautum: Happy is he
that

stand you beneath him, as the water runneth, so that you may angle in the thicke water, and you shall haue trim sporte, and if he that doth stirre the water, haue in a bag of linnen some ground malt, and now & then cast in as muche as he may hold betweene his three fingers, where hee stirreth, that it may fall iust where you angle, it is the better, and you may put on two hoks at this sporte, & so haue a good messe quickly, land when you see the bite die, then remoue to another place, & so on, as your store of fish, plats, and speeding is.

Vi. Nowe commeth your wife againe, and I shalbe shent for keping you from eating.

Pi. No, no, she knoweth this talk to be meat and drink vnto me. Now wife, come and sit downe.

Ci. We haue brought you all.

C.b.   Vi.

Ui. All quoth ye: In deede here is
ftoze, O here is the great Pearche
that you tooke in the mozning, it is
fo in deed. But what are thefe lying
about him.

Pi. Ruffes.

Ui. What fiſhe is it?

Pi. Oh excellent.

Ui. I praye you howe take you
them?

Ci. Good ſir let him eat his meate.

Pi. My wife counteth me like the
inſtrument of Lincolneſhere.   But
now that I haue fome what ſtayed
my hunger, I can bothe eate & talk.
The ruffe is the groſeſt at his bit of
any fiſh that biteth & is taken with
the red wozme on the grounde, and
where he lieth there is he commonly
alone, he is enuious, brifteled on the
backe as y Pearch, in ech fin a ſharp
pricke, his gilles ſharpe at the ende,
and ſwalloweth the bait at the firſt,

great

great goggled eyed, and cōmeth vp
very churlishly, and will holde his
lippes so heard together, that you
shal haue much a do to open them, &
commonly you must rend the gilles
a sunder to get out your hooke, he is
full of blacke spots, and like to rised
baken, and therefore we cal them lit=
tle hogs, but surely an holsome fish,
With two haires you may fishe for
him, he is so grose in his feeding, &
commeth not vppe gently, holde you
there is one of them, tast of him and
tell me.

Ui. A very good fish.

Pi. There can not be a better, and
chiefly for a sicke body, I count him
better than either goodgiō or perch,
for he eateth faster and pleasanter,
the onely worme is his baite that e=
uer I did knowe, my Maister that
taught me to angle, could not abide
to catch a Ruffe, for if he toke one, ei=
the

ther he would remoue, or wind vp a
home for that time, he did knowe thē
so masterly among other fish, but for
my part, I haue beene well content
to deale with them, for this proper-
tie they haue, as is seene among the
wicked, that thoughe they see their
fellowes perish neuer so fast, yet will
they not be warned, so that you shal
haue them as long as one is lefte,
especially a little before a raine, or in
the bite time. And if you close some
small wormes in a ball of olde black
doung or earth, and cast it in where
you angle for them you shall haue the
better sport, for at the will they lie like
little hogges, as is aforesaid. You so
listē to my talk that you eat nothing

Ti. You men say that women bee
talkatiue, but here is suche a number of words about nothing, as passeth.

Pi. Why so I say, all is nothing
with

with you and your kinde , vnlesse it
be about pinnes and laces, frindge
and gards, fine linnen and wollen,
hats and hat bandes , gloues, and
scarffes : and yet J meruaile that
you shoulde say that my talke hathe
beene of nothing.for one part of the
tyre that now is of no small charge a
mong you,we haue a fishe to father
it, called a Ruffe, of whom J spake
euen nowe , vnlesse you will haue it
the diminutiue of a Ruffian , but it
may be that the name doth come frō
the ruffe the fish, for surely the greater part that vse the long gut gathered together of this fishe, they maye
well be said to be in their ruffe , and
like vnto the ruffe in disdaine.

   Vi. Well, now J pray you to the
taking of the Pearch.

   Pi. The Pearch is a grose fishe &
easily taken, a red worme is his common baite, but the quick Menow is
the

the best putting your hooke thorow
the corner of her lip, and so let her
swimme aliue an ell in the water,
with plumbets to keep her down, &
strike not ouer soone whē you see the
bit, but let him goe as farre as the
length of your line, that he may swal
low it, or else his mouthe is so wide,
and so full of bones, and also he will
many times gape for the nonce, and
cast out hooke and menow. The menow, the menow also will somwhat
beare off your hooke, but when your
fish is in his gullet, then all is safe,
so that your hooke bend not, or your
line breake.

Vi. I may fishe with mō hairs for
him than one or two.

Vi. That you may with foure or
fire, and a good handsome compassed
hook, he will also in winter bite at a
good gentill, or a ball of bread, a ra-
uenous fish it is also, and liueth for
the

the most part by eating vp of his fel
lowes, as the couetous inclosers do,
and if you come to the laire of greate
Pearches, let your line be strong, for
when you haue striken one, the residue wil come and make suche a stir
about your line and him, with their
bristelles vp, that they will deliuer
their fellow, if you haue not a good
line and very good holde.

Vi. Why then they be like to hogs
& both better than most men, whiche
seeing their neighbour in trouble,
will rather helpe to keepe him in
trouble, then to worke to bring him
out. But be these al the baites that
do belong to the taking of a pearch?

Pi. No, he will bite very well at
the red knotted woorme: yea and at a
yellow frushe or frog, if it bee a little
one, and a small goodgion is very
good, but ý great knotted red worm
(well ordered and well put on the
hooke

hoke, as we vse to do foz the Cheuin,
is a special good bayte.

Ui. How meane you the ozdering?

Pi. As foz that, J will tell you in
the ende foz the ozdering of all your
baytes.

Ui. Then J pzay you to the Pickrell.

Pi. The Pickrell is also a fleſhie
fiſhe, and liueth by rauening and eating of his fellowes, and beareth the
ſwinge of the fiſhes, and is called the
freſhwater wolfe, groſe witted, hath
a weede of his owne, which alſo hee
will feede on, called Pickrell weede,
he wil be haltered, and ſome men vſe
that way very oft to kill him, foz hee
wil lie ſtaring vpon you, as the hare
oz larke, vntil you put the line with
a ſnittel ouer his head, and ſo with
a good ſtiff pole you may thzow him
to land: this way is beſt in ſtanding
waters and pooles.

Ui.

Ui. This is a carterly rude way,
I pray you tell me howe to kill him
with an angle?

Pi. He is so grose a rauener as I
said, that any thing will kill him, for
he will bite at a ientell, if it come in
his mad head, but then your hook is
gon he will shere so with his teeth.
When you fish for him, you must fish
with an armed hook of three lincks,
and your line of sixteene or twentie
haires, & a good big floate, a double
hook, & a handsom Roch or Dace,
or Frogge, he wilbe killed with a
great red worme as I haue proued.

Ui. How shal I put on my Roch,
or my frog?

Pi. You must rippell with your
point of your knife ouerthwart the
Roch vnder the gill, that the scales
and skinne may be taken away and
opened, and then put in the ende
your arming, and so thrust it downe

D.   the

the side of the Roch betweene ẏ flesh
and the skinne, and let it come out at
the taile of the fish, so drawing your
lincks of arming gentily, vntill the
hook be nothing seen but ẏ bearded
points vnder hir gill, then put your
line on, and let your flote be of cozke,
& not passing an el frõ your fish, this
bait after this maner may be either
legger oz a walker, foz if you either
be wery oz would sit down and loke
on a booke, oz mend your geres, oz
with an other angle fish foz Roch oz
Pearch thereby, you may, thzowing
your bait as farre into the water as
you may with a long line, and lay
downe your rod on the banke : but
looke to the bit & be not far off, least
that either your pole oz cane, be pulled in with some good fishe, oz that
when she hath stroken her selfe (foz
so she will with swallowing the bait
into her gullet) that she get not into
the wede, as among the cane rotes,

& cloſſer leaues, oʒ her owne weede, &
thē ſhal you neuer get her out woout
a boate, and a rede hooke, vnleſſe the
weeds be by the bāks ſide, & then wo
a peece of packethʒead tying your
knife at the ende of your Pike angle,
making it like a weede hooke, you
may ſhʒed the weeds vnder the fiſh,
ſo may you come vp fiſh and hooke.

Vi. Is there any other way to fiſh
foʒ the Pickrel?

Pi. Yea, as I ſaie, as by walking
and fiſhiug with a dead baite, and
ſpecially a bleke, though ſhe be a day
olde, and laid againſt the ſunne, oʒ
carried betweene the crowne of your
head and the top of your hat, to dʒie
the ſooner, thʒee oʒ foure, and put
your hook thoʒow her noſe oʒ nether
lip, and ſo walke the Riuer, and let
it neuer ſtand ſtil, but be mouing of
it vp and downe, and ſtill dʒawing,
but not haſtily and when you ſee the

ſlote

flote pulled at, and sinke, let him goe as long as you may, for he wil some time carrie the bait ouerthwart his mouth, a good while, or euer that he wil swallow it, and especially, if that he haue been striken at before, & hardly scaped, and a good fish. Also the Frog is a very good baite, the yelower the better, and the head of an Eele, and a good big goodgion quick

Ci. You eate no meate nowe, therfore it may be taken away.

Pi. In deede as you know wife, it is better to fill my belly than mine eye, and a litle thing doth suffise nature, and this talke is for my turne.

Ui. Well then, if it please you let vs haue a cup of sack, and an apple, or a peare, and then let vs rise a Gods name.

Pi. Not so, for I loue to take mine ease in myne Inn, & yet a bit or two more. Reache wife that other dishe neere me.   Ui.

Vi. What fiche is this I pray you
in the middes?

Pi. It is a Chob,and would haue
bin within this yeare a Cheuin, say
I pray you a morsell of him : those y
lye about him are Roches.

Vi. It is a sweete fich, but he eateth somewhat flachly, and is full of
bones.

Ci. In deed Syr ye say true, and
therefore either I dare not lette my
children eate of that fiche, or else I
giue them great charge to take heed
of bones, and when they eate of the
pickrell also. But for this fiche my
husband hathe no greate pleasure in
them, and if he doe bring any home,
he will not eat of them if hee haue a-
ny other fiche.

Pi. I doe not much passe of any
fiche to eate, but that hunger forceth
mee sometimes and want of other
things,and when I am wearie (as

it

it were) of flesh: and yet the Cheuins head I do loue very well, for nexte vnto the Carpes head, it is the best, and very sweet, if the mouth be clean washed. But or euer I speake any further of him, I must tell you a storie of the age of a luse or pike, which Gesnerus doth make report of with a Ring about his necke, of this fashion here after drawne.

In the yeare of our Lorde 1497. a Pike was taken in a lake about Haslepurn the imperial citie of Swethland, and a ring of copper found in his gilles vnder his skin, and a little part thereof seene shining, whose figure and inscription about the compasse of it was such in greeke as we here exhibite: whiche John Dalburg Bishop of worms did expound it thus. I am the first fish of all, put into this lake by the handes of Frederick the second, ruler of the world.

The

The fifth day of October, in the yere of our Lord M.CC.and xxx.Therevpon is gathered the summe of CC. lx.& vii.yeares. And verily before it was of Frederick the Emperour so marked, a good while it had liued, & if as yet it had not bin taken, it wold haue liued a longer time.

And now to return to the Cheuin, when I dwelled in Sauoye, the ouermost parts of Zwitzerlande, in angling in a part of Losana lake, & the ditch of Geneua, but chiefly in $\tilde{y}$ swift Rodanus, I tooke sometime the Cheuin and very faire, the people marueiling at my pastime (for that recreation is not there vsed) they much more marueled that I,or any of my countrimen woulde eate of them, for they do as much despise them, as the Frieser in Frieslande, doth abhorre to eate Calues fleſh.

Vi. How kill you the Cheuin?

D.iiii.   Pi.

The Arte

Pi. He will bite very well at a Menowe, the great red wozme, the white wozme in the dead Alhe, the grashopper, ý yong vnhaired mouse, the blacke snaile slit in the back, that her grease may hang out, the hoznet, the great beare wozme in a swifte streame, oz at a mylltayle, with heauie geres, the marrowe in the ridge bone of a loyne of veale, yea and rather then fayle, at a piece of bacon, I meane the fat.

Ui. I haue heard say, that he wil not sticke to bite at a frog.

Pi. I knowe not that, but this I tell you, you must stand close, foz hee hath a quick eye, and wil flie like an arrowe out of a bowe to his den oz hole, whiche he is neuer farre from: your line must be strong, and your hoke wel hardened. Well, now after grace we wil sit by the fire.

Ui. And haue an other fitte.

Pi.

of Angling.

Pi. Sometime with all the cunning that we haue, wee come home without, and take such as we finde, and not such as we bring, and then should we haue best cheere made vs.

Ui. And why? for mee thinketh that then you do deserue worst.

Pi. Nay not so, for that were a double hurt, bothe to haue euill luck abrode, and worse at home, but as it is with hunters, so is it with vs, for their rule is to fare best, when they speede not: the one reason why: is this, that then they haue taken most and longest paine: an other is, that so are they well comforted after their vnspeeding sporte, and by that meanes incouraged the rather to go to it againe, to make some recompence. But what do I among hunters, if one of thē heard me, he would say Ne vltra sutor crepidam. Say grace maide.

D.b.   Anne

Anne. The GOD of peace which brought againe from, &c.

Pi. Nowe to the fire, get him a chaire, and nowe will wee speake of angling for the Carpe. He is a stout headie fish, strōg headed and tailed, and mightily boned and scaled, a fish not long knowen in Englande, but very deintie, & specially well baked, for then may ye eate him bones and all.

Vi. Will he bite as well as other fishe?

Pi. Yea, but as his layre is, for if he be in a pond, he wil bite al sum-mer in a manner, sauing in shelrode time, which some cal spauning time, which time is forbidden to fish for a-ny kinde of fishe, he is not in many Riuers, it hath not beene hearde of that the Carpe hath beene found in any running water or streame, but by heds of poles bursting out, wher

Carpes

Carpes haue beene, oz land floudes
that haue ouerflowed such places, &
so they haue ben carried into riuers
as I know a Riuer my selfe, where
beyond sirteene yeres past there was
neuer heard of noz seene any Carpe,
by the oldest man, and now there be
so many, that it is no newes foz one
man with his angle to kil in a mozning twentie oz foztie, yea there is
such stoze that foz my part I would
there were fewer, they beare such a
sway in the Riuer, that all other fish
are almost gone. They may be compared to some stout needy vpstarts,
foz thoughe they can not rauen and
destroy their fellowes (vnlesse it be
a pooze Menowe) yet with counte-
naunce & shouldering, other fish will
not gladly be where they abounde.
Their first comming into this Riuer, was surely by some great flood,
whiche came out of Buckingham
shyze

there & Bedfordshere, which sheeres
are well furnished with Carps; but
nowe haue they setteled them selues
with vs, & do breede, so that at some
rising of waters beneath vs, they do
take them in by diches by coulefuls,
of a span long & vpward, our fennes
be now full, you shall haue an C. of
goodly store fish, of one foote a peece
in length for fiue shillings.

Vi. Well now I pray you to the
taking of him.

Pi. In the Riuer he will bite,
chiefly in August & all September,
his bit is in the morning, and late
at the night. I know but two baits
for him, y one is the great red worm
the other is bread, some say, new baked Rie bread, and some say, white
bread, but this I do knowe by experience, that looke what bread you vse
him to in feeding of him, that shal ye
take him with all.

Vi.

Vi. Why must you feede him?

Pi. Yea that you must, either in poole oz running Riuer, thoughe in the fennes there is suche stoze, that where any little voide plotte is foz leaues, you cannot put in your baite amisse, as I haue heard.

Vi. But I pzay you how shall I feede them?

Pi. You must take with you a good shiuer of bzead, in a faire linnē bag oz cloth, and when you come to your place, take a peece and chewe it in your mouth vntill it be moist, and then ball it, and cast it in where your flote shalbe, & so two oz thzee mouths full if you wil, whiles you are a ma= king of your tooles readie, then bait your hooke with the same chewed bzed, this added to, that that which you bait withal, be laboured in your pauline of your left hande, with the thumb of your right hand, but looke
that

that it be neither too tough, nor too brittell, for they be bothe hurtfull.

Vi. Howe so?

Pi. If the baite be tough and hardish, like stiffe dow, then it is to hard for the hooke to goe easily thorowe, specially when the bit is not fast, and so the fishe letteth it go as it came, or grateth a litle in her mouthe, and so hurteth the pastime, the toughnes of the bread pulling it off, that the hooke cannot fully strike at the first, vnlesse you strike hard, and that againe is daungerous, for breaking of your line, tearing of her lip, knapping asunder of the small end of your angle, and last of all the souden mouing of the water, with the sight of your geares, whiche wil make the fishe shoye, and fearefull.

Vi. What other bait haue you for him?

Pi. The greate worme is also a
good

good bait as J said, lying a foote on the ground, as the bread must, and a bob of gentils, he wil bite at some time.

Ui. When biteth he best?

Pt. J told you, in August & Septēb. strike not vntil you see him go away with the baite by pulling downe of your flote, and if your bready bait be brittle, as mingled with barley, oz not wel kneeded in your hand, then the small fishe wil nible it off. Thus haue J spoken of the killing of the Carp in the Riuer, and in the ponde oz mote, the baites afoze be good, so that you meate a plat oz two oz moe as you shall thinke good, euening & mozning with bread, graines and bloud mingled together, oz ground malt, and cut with a long pole and a hooke the weedes away a good cō-passe, foz feare of his running in to them: and be sure that your line bee

strong,

strong, as of green silke, or haire, of xvi. or xx. haires in the line. In the pond he will bite at all times in the summer, sauing in shelrode time, as I saide.

Vi. But Sir, I pray you, what bait haue you for killing of the house Carpe? nowe you haue spoken of the riuer Carpe and pond Carpe?

Pi. The best baite that euer I did know for the killing of þ Carpe, is, a quantitie of sufferance, with a good deale of patience, and as much silence as may be possible, all these well mingled togither, and so goe your way, if you see that there be no remedie.

Vi. Why, some holde that those carpes are best killed with an angle made of an hasell wande, without a line.

Pi. In deede some do vse it, but whither they kill the Carpes or
catch

catch moze Carpes that way oz no,
that I haue no experience off, & ther
foze can fay litle.

Ui. Well, I knowe fome, that if
they ſhould not vſe that kind of angling, they ſhold not be without ſtoze
of Carpes, both at bed and at bozde.

Pi. Yea, but then they bee cloyde
with pouts, which is an il fauoured
fiſh: and if ther be no remedie, rather
giue me the Carpe, than the poute,
although I like neither, foz the head
of the one is better than the liuer of
the other. But nowe to leaue this
kinde of carping, let vs now paſſe on
to ſpeake further of angling.

Ui. Contente, howe kill you the
Bzeame?

Pi. At the ground with a redde
wozm, the ientill, bzowne bzead, and
the oke wozme: he is heady & heauy,
but ſoone checked: he biteth but ſeldome, and that deintily, loth to bee
hurt, & flieth if you miſſe him with

E.   tou-

touching, as J will tell you a straūg tale of a bзeame that was taken in oure Riuer, called the Ouse, which bзeaine J bought.

Ui. Was she taken in a nette, oz with an angle?

Pi. With a nett in dзawing the water at Huntington bзidge, & whē she should be put into a trunk (as J willed foz a time to bee kept aliue) the hole was with the least, foz shee was a very great fishe, of a bзeame, bothe in bзedth and thicknesse, as e-uer J sawe, and so with strougling, she slipped into the water, and away she went, whiche grieued mee some-what.

Ui. J blaine you not.

Pi. Yet God sent her mee againe, foz within thзee oz foure dayes after warde the water beneathe vs also was dзawne at a towne called saint Tyues, thзee myle from vs by land, but foure good mile by water, and

there

there was that self same breame taken again, and so I was faine to bye
her the second time.

Ui. But I pray you howe did you
know that it was shee & none other?

Pi. By two markes, one was that
on the side of her head vnder the gil,
she had a great red wen, as broade
as a testor, and also I had cut off a
piece of her taile.

Ui. Now surely it was straunge.

Pi. It was so, for I haue seene
the contrary in other fishe, as once I
did see a good pearch stricken, & long
tuggid with all, and when shee was
teady to be landed, the ouer end of y
hoke had so fretted the haire, that it
brake, and away shee went, and the
party fastening on an other hoke,
layd in agayn, and surely within an
hower after, the same Pearche did
byte agayne, he stroke her, and had
her with the hoke in her lip, that she
had gon away withall afore: with

E.ii.   which

which two examples I haue learned, that some fishe hath better me-
morie than othersome haue, or one
more fearefull than another.

Ui. I haue heard of another bayte
or twain that is good for the bream.

Pi. Ye say true, the flag worme,
and the bob vnder the cow torde.

Ui. The flag worme, howe come
you by hir?

Pi. You must pul vp flags by the
rootes out of the water, and in the
rootes you shal finde white wormes
as big as gentils, and they be very
good: yea I may say to you, for the
Carpe also, but that euery body may
not know it, for that is a secret. And
in the rootes of the rushe you shall
finde good baytes also. But nowe to
the Dace.

Ui. Well sayd, I pray you how do
you angle for him?

Pi. Two wayes, aboue and beneath: for from June vntil Septē-
ber

ber, hee will bite aboue at the flie,
without led oz flote, oz with a small
quill without lead, and within two
fote of the flie. You must haue a long
line, you must stand close and throw
with the wind and with the streame,
your eye being very good, and a rea=
dy hand, with a long hazell wand, oz
other trim straight wand, foz a rede
is not good.

Vi. How many hairs at that hoke
must I haue?

Pi. You may haue twoo oz three
haires, because that your stroke, the
swift bit of the fish, and against the
streame, as you must strike, the line
had neede be of some strength, & the
fish must also be considered: foz if you
come amóg great Daces (as I haue
seene some as big as a fresh herring
ful) then shal you find iii. hairs with
the least, and they had neede to bee
good, wel twisted, & without frets.

Vi. They may not be shee haires
then?   C.iii.   Pi.

Pi. No in deede, foz they bee not good, they be so often moisted, neyther is ẙ gelding haire so good, but of these matters hereafter. After September, vntil the middes of Febzuarie, at the very grounð, he will byte, either at the red wozme, ientill, oke wozme, oz malt cozn, yea at the very grounð, trayling on it in a grauely place is best, ᵹ thē w one haire.

Ui. Why, all those months be in a maner winter moneths, and I had thought that then pour angles had shzouded.

Pi. No, no then is the chiefest angling. I haue on twelfth euen, ᵹ on Candlemas euen taken such messes of fish with mine angle, as hath passed: yea in frost ᵹ snow when the yce sickles hath hanged at mine angle top, I haue had best spozte. When he bytes, if you light of the skull, hee bytes sure, and is a headdy fishe to land, ᵹ if he wzestle with you, haue
him

him out of your plat as much as you
may to tire him, for hurting of your
gaine. Well now to the Roche.

Ui. How kill you her?

Pi. In summer with the red worm,
vntil it be about Michelmasse, and
then the malt corne, and after the len=
til, that fish is the common fish and ea=
sily killed: she is very simple, and the
plat being well meated with balles,
you shall fil your paile at a plat, if the
scar come not.

Ui. What is that?

Pi. The Pike or pickrel.

Ui. How shall I knowe, when hee
is come?

Pi. By casting in of your meate,
which may be vnballed if the water
be still, for immediatly after, you shal
see the small fishe flie soudenly euery
way, and sometimes aboue the wa=
ter, and he after.

Ui. Then the sport is marred?

Pi. That is true, but for euery

E.iiii.   sore

fore there is a falue. You muſt haue
a pike hook ready, and put on a ſmal
Roche with a good ſtrong line, and
a flote, hauing a ſpare rod by you,
and caſte it in, and let it lie by you
vntil he bite, & ſo ſhall you haue him:
It may be that your ſport is hurt al
ſo with a great pearch or two, and
then a goodgion or a menno is be-
ry good w a ſtrong ſingle hoke caſt in
with a ſpare rod lying by you, as before. But in winter, as about Chriſt-
maſſe, Candlemaſſe, & Lent, if water be not froſen ouer, vntil the fiſhe
goe to rode, the red worme is very
good, but chiefly, the white worme
that breedeth betweene the barke &
the wood of an oke, with a litle red
hard head. In ſtocks of oke that ſtad
vpright or lie dye, they commonly
be, which haue ben two yeres felled.
And ſometimes you ſhal haue them
in the wood, and thoſe be commonly
great and faire : then muſt you rend
them out.   Di.

WS - #0080 - 131124 - C0 - 229/152/9 - PB - 9780282553913 - Gloss Lamination